HAMMOND
Historical World Atlas

A collection of maps illustrating the most significant periods and events in history from the dawn of civilization to the present day.

Contents

HISTORICAL WORLD MAP SERIES

CONTEMPORANEOUS CULTURES, CIVILIZATIONS, STATES AND EMPIRES

The World in:
500 B.C., Persian Empire and Greece I
323 B.C., Alexander's empire at his death I
200 B.C., Successor states to Alexander's empires; Asoka's Empire ... II
14 A.D., Early Roman Empire; Han Dynasty; early American groups ... II
200 A.D., Roman Empire near its greatest extent;
  Empires connected by the "Silk Route" III
420 A.D., Roman Empire splits into Eastern and Western sections;
  China divided; Ghana appears; Mayan States III
600 A.D., Eastern Roman Empire at greatest extent;
  beginnings of Frankish realm IV
800 A.D., The extensive reach of Islam; China's Tang Dynasty;
  Frankish Empire under Charlemagne IV
1000 A.D., Beginnings of European states V
1237 A.D., Unified Mongol Empire before the invasion of Russia;
  new realms in Africa and America V
1300 A.D., Successor realms to Mongol Empire VI
1400 A.D., Beginnings of Ottoman Empire; Ming Dynasty VI
1519 A.D., Spanish Empire in New World; Inca Empire;
  Portuguese outposts in Africa and Asia VII
1600 A.D., Spanish and Ottoman Empires at greatest extent;
  Moroccan Empire VII
1714 A.D., Russian Empire extends eastward,
  British Colonies in North America; Moguls dominate India VIII
1804 A.D., United States after Louisiana Purchase;
  Habsburg monarch becomes Emperor of Austria
  (end of Holy Roman Empire) VIII

ERAS AND TURNING POINTS IN THE HISTORY OF CULTURES, CIVILIZATIONS, STATES AND EMPIRES

Prehistoric Man H-2
The Spread of Farming and Early Domestication
  of Crops and Animals H-2
The Cradles of Civilization, 3000–1000 B.C. H-3
Major States and Empires in 500 B.C. H-3
Major States and Empires in 400 A.D. H-3
The Expansion of Western Civilization, 1600 A.D. H-3
Middle Eastern Cradlelands c. 1350 B.C. H-4
  a. Early Empires of Mesopotamia, 2371–1750 B.C.
The Assyrian Empire, 824 to 625 B.C. H-5
Great Empires of the Sixth Century B.C. H-5
The Biblical World H-6
Ancient Greece (Hellas) H-6
  a. Ancient Athens   b. Crete
Asia, 250–200 B.C. H-7
  a. Indus Valley Civilization, 2400–1500 B.C.
  b. Shang Dynasty China, 1600–1027 B.C.
The Persian Empire and the Empire of Alexander the Great H-8
The Roman Empire about 117 A.D. H-8
Ancient Italy before Augustus H-9
  a. The Forum, Capitolium and Palatium   b. Imperial Fora
  c. Environs of Rome   d. Rome under the Emperors
  e. Rome in the Time of the Republic
Eurasia, 100 A.D. H-10
  a. The Known World
Eurasia, 450 A.D. H-10
  a. India, 640 A.D.
Europe showing Barbarian Migrations in the IV and V Centuries H-11
Europe, 600 A.D. H-12
Europe c. 800 A.D. H-13
  a. Treaty of Verdun, 843   b. Treaty of Mersen, 870   c. Final Partition
Britannia about 350 A.D. H-14
English Conquest from 450 to End of the VI Century H-14
England in the VIII Century (The "Heptarchy") H-14
England after the Peace of Wedmore (878 A.D.) H-14
The Expansion of Islam, 622-700 A.D. H-15
The Expansion of Islam, 700-900 A.D. H-15
Europe and the Byzantine Empire about 1000 A.D. H-16
Mediterranean Lands in 1097 .... H-17
  a. The Califate in 750
Mediterranean Lands after 1204 .... H-17
  a. Latin States in Syria
Historical Map of Asia H-18

Europe c. 1200 A.D. H-19
Ecclesiastical Map of Europe c. 1300 A.D. H-20
Economic Map of Europe in the Middle Ages, 1300 A.D. H-21
English Possessions in France, 1066 to 1272 .... H-22
France at the Death of Philip IV (The Fair), 1314 .... H-22
France at the Peace of Bretigny, 1360 .... H-22
France at the Death of Henry V, 1422 .... H-22
The Principal Voyages of Discovery to America, 1492-1611 .... H-23
Europe in 1559 .... H-24
Europe in 1648 at the Peace of Westphalia H-25
Europe in 1713-1714 at the Treaties of Utrecht and Rastatt H-26
Changing Ownership of the Continent (North America) H-26
  a. 1682   b. 1713   c. 1763   d. 1783
French and Indian War, 1756 to 1763 .... H-26
  a. The Principal Battleground of the French and Indian War
Europe in 1763 .... H-27
Poland to 1667 .... H-28
Poland–Result of the 1st Partition, 1772 .... H-28
Poland–Result of the 2nd Partition, 1793 .... H-28
Poland–Result of the 3rd Partition, 1795 .... H-28
France at the Outbreak of the Revolution–Inequalities of the Salt Tax .. H-29
Paris at the Outbreak of the Revolution H-29
Western Germany at the Outbreak of the French Revolution H-30
Europe in 1803 .... H-30
Europe in 1812 at the Height of Napoleon's Power H-31
Europe after the Congress of Vienna, 1815 to 1839 .... H-32
The Colonization of Latin America H-33
Latin American Countries since the Colonial Period H-33
Italy at the Close of the XV Century H-34
Unification of Italy, 1859 to 1924 .... H-34
Central Europe, 1815 to 1871 .... H-35
The Peoples of Europe, 1910 .... H-35
England before the Industrial Revolution, c. 1701 .... H-36
England after the Industrial Revolution H-36
The Growth of the Ottoman Empire, 1299–1672 .... H-37
The Decline of the Ottoman Empire, 1699–1923 .... H-37
The Growth of Russia, covering the period from 1054 to 1914 .... H-38
Russian-British rivalry, 1801–1914 .... H-39
China and the Major Powers, 1841–1914 .... H-39
Early Africa, 4500 B.C. to 1000 A.D. H-40
African Kingdoms and Empires, 750 B.C.–1901 A.D. H-40
European Exploration of Africa, 1455–1900 .... H-40
Africa 1885 .... H-40
Africa in 1914 .... H-41
Asia in 1914 .... H-41
Voyages of Discovery to Australia and New Zealand 1606–1799 .... H-42
Exploration of Australia, 1803–1879 .... H-42
Australian Settlement H-42
Australian Territorial Changes, 1788–1931 .... H-42
Exploration of Canada, 1497–1906 .... H-43
The Growth of Canada from 1791 to 1949 .... H-43
Europe in 1914 .... H-44
The First World War, 1914–1918 .... H-45
  a. Europe and the Near East   b. The Western Front
Europe, 1919 to 1929 .... H-46
The World, 1919 to 1938, Major Powers and Nations
  with Overseas Territories H-47
Europe, 1930 to 1939 .... H-48
The Far East, 1930 to 1941 .... H-48
The World at War, 1939 to 1945 .... H-49
European Theatre of War, 1939 to 1945 .... H-50
Far Eastern Theatre of War, 1941 to 1945 .... H-50
Europe in 1941 .... H-51
Europe during the Cold War, 1945 to 1989 .... H-52
Present Day Europe H-52
Europe–Physical H-53
The Middle East since 1945 .... H-54
South and East Asia since 1945 .... H-55
The Korean War, 1950–1953 .... H-56
The Vietnam Conflict, 1959–1975 .... H-56
Africa since 1945 .... H-57
Middle America since 1945 .... H-58
The Retreat of Colonialism in the Post-War Period 1945–1990 .... H-59
The World of the United Nations and the Cold War 1945–1990 .... H-60
The Population Explosion and World Urbanization H-61
Rich Nations vs. Poor Nations: Gross National Product H-62
Global Relationships in the 1990's H-63
Time Charts–A Graphic History of Mankind .... H-64 through H-71
The Present Day World-Political Map H-72

HAMMOND World Atlas Corporation
Revised 2003 Edition © 2000 Hammond World Atlas Corporation

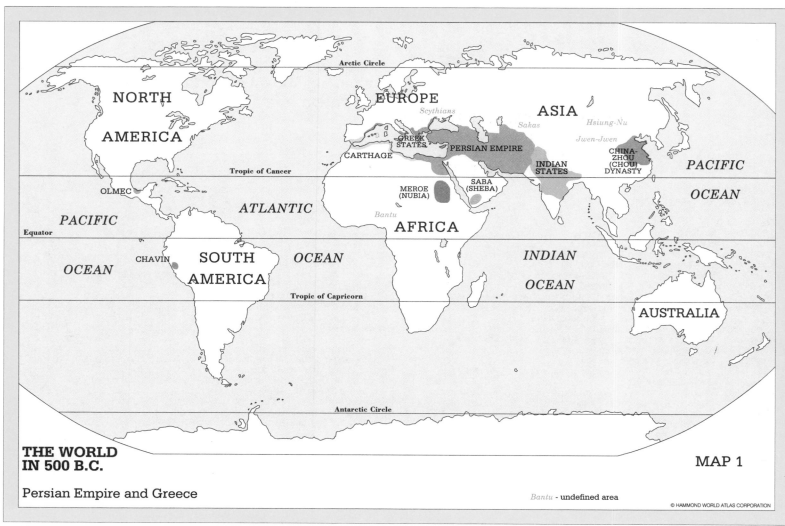

NORTH
AMERICA

EUROPE
Scythians

ASIA

Sakas

Hsiung-Nu

Jwen-Jwen

GREEK
STATES

PERSIAN EMPIRE

INDIAN
STATES

CHINA-
ZHOU
(CHOU)
DYNASTY

PACIFIC

CARTHAGE

OCEAN

Tropic of Cancer

OLMEC

ATLANTIC

MEROE
(NUBIA)

SABA
(SHEBA)

Bantu

AFRICA

Equator

PACIFIC

SOUTH
AMERICA

OCEAN

INDIAN

CHAVIN

OCEAN

OCEAN

Tropic of Capricorn

AUSTRALIA

Arctic Circle

Antarctic Circle

**THE WORLD
IN 500 B.C.**

MAP 1

Persian Empire and Greece

Bantu - undefined area

© HAMMOND WORLD ATLAS CORPORATION

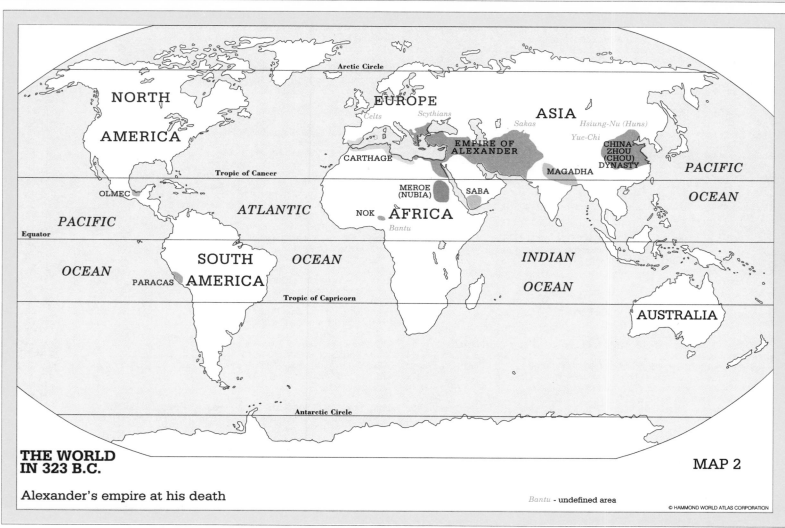

NORTH
AMERICA

EUROPE

Celts

Scythians

ASIA

Sakas

Hsiung-Nu (Huns)

Yue-Chi

EMPIRE OF
ALEXANDER

CHINA-
ZHOU
(CHOU)
DYNASTY

CARTHAGE

MAGADHA

PACIFIC

Tropic of Cancer

OLMEC

OCEAN

PACIFIC

ATLANTIC

MEROE
(NUBIA)

SABA

NOK

AFRICA

Bantu

Equator

OCEAN

SOUTH
AMERICA

OCEAN

INDIAN

PARACAS

OCEAN

Tropic of Capricorn

AUSTRALIA

Arctic Circle

Antarctic Circle

**THE WORLD
IN 323 B.C.**

MAP 2

Alexander's empire at his death

Bantu - undefined area

© HAMMOND WORLD ATLAS CORPORATION

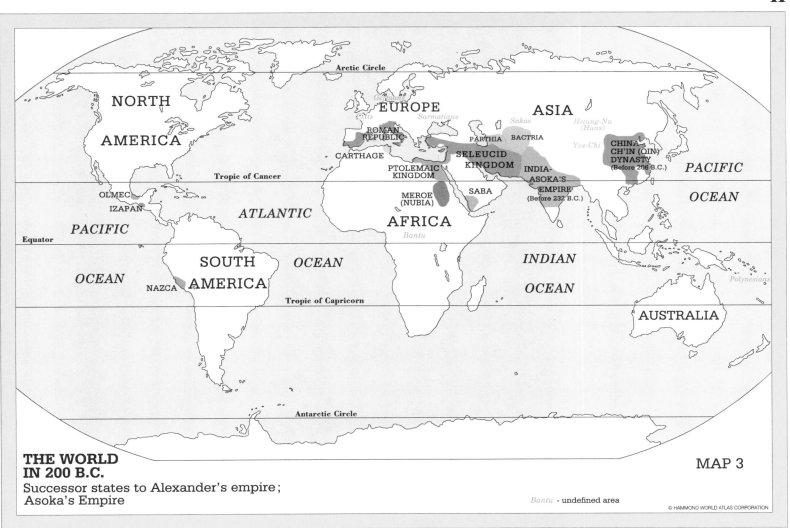

**THE WORLD
IN 200 B.C.**

Successor states to Alexander's empire;
Asoka's Empire

MAP 3

Bantu - undefined area

© HAMMOND WORLD ATLAS CORPORATION

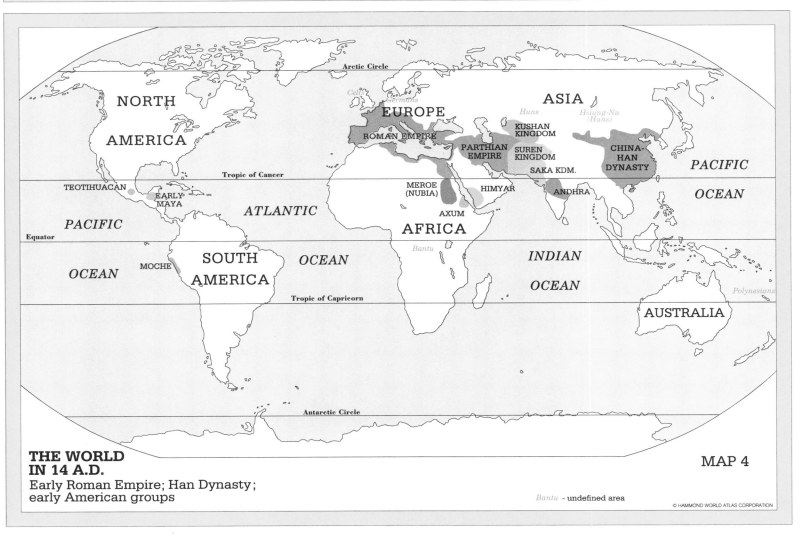

**THE WORLD
IN 14 A.D.**

Early Roman Empire; Han Dynasty;
early American groups

MAP 4

Bantu - undefined area

© HAMMOND WORLD ATLAS CORPORATION

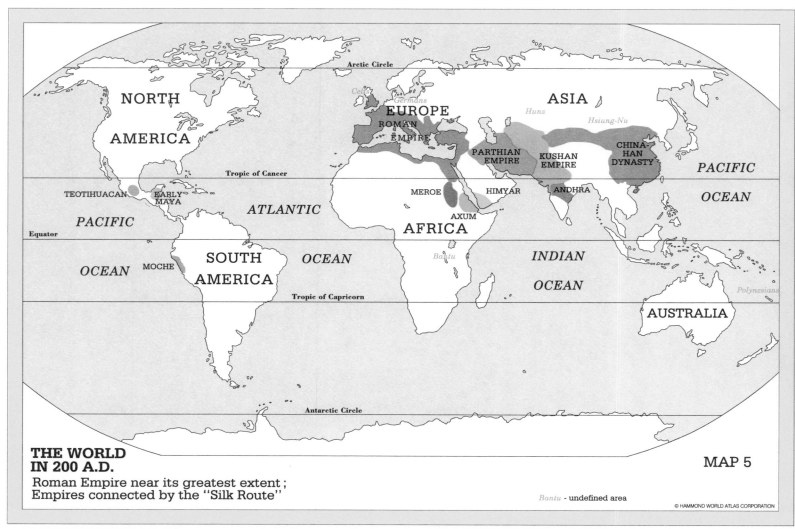

NORTH
AMERICA

Celts
Germans
EUROPE
**ROMAN
EMPIRE**
Huns
ASIA
Hsiung-Nu

Arctic Circle

Tropic of Cancer

TEOTIHUACAN
EARLY
MAYA

**PARTHIAN
EMPIRE**
**KUSHAN
EMPIRE**
**CHINA-
HAN
DYNASTY**

PACIFIC

MEROE
HIMYAR
ANDHRA

OCEAN

ATLANTIC
AFRICA
AXUM

PACIFIC
Equator
OCEAN

OCEAN
MOCHE
SOUTH
AMERICA
OCEAN
Bantu
INDIAN

OCEAN
Tropic of Capricorn

AUSTRALIA

Polynesians

Antarctic Circle

**THE WORLD
IN 200 A.D.**

MAP 5

Roman Empire near its greatest extent ;
Empires connected by the "Silk Route"

Bantu - undefined area

© HAMMOND WORLD ATLAS CORPORATION

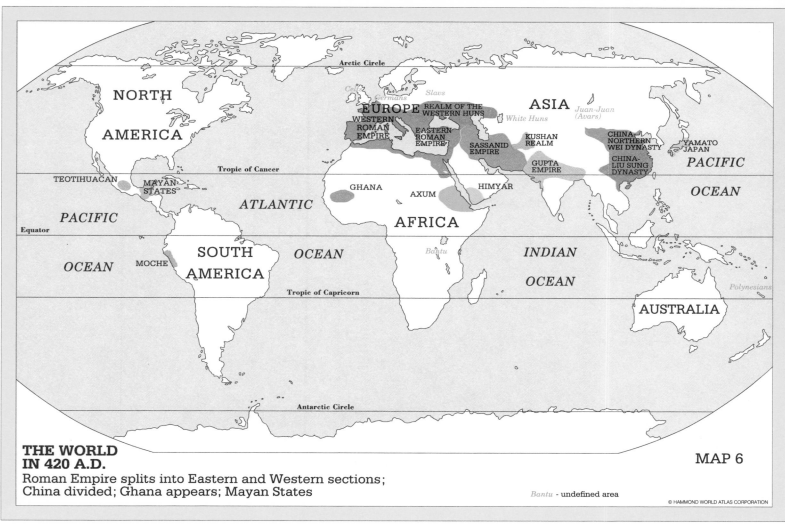

NORTH
AMERICA

Celts
Germans
Slavs
EUROPE
**REALM OF THE
WESTERN HUNS**
ASIA
*Juan-Juan
(Avars)*

Arctic Circle

**WESTERN
ROMAN
EMPIRE**
White Huns

Tropic of Cancer

TEOTIHUACAN
**MAYAN
STATES**

**EASTERN
ROMAN
EMPIRE**
**SASSANID
EMPIRE**
**KUSHAN
REALM**
**CHINA-
NORTHERN
WEI DYNASTY**
**YAMATO
JAPAN**

GHANA
AXUM
HIMYAR
**GUPTA
EMPIRE**
**CHINA-
LIU SUNG
DYNASTY**

PACIFIC

ATLANTIC
AFRICA
OCEAN

PACIFIC
Equator
OCEAN
MOCHE
SOUTH
AMERICA
OCEAN
Bantu
INDIAN

OCEAN
Tropic of Capricorn

AUSTRALIA

Polynesians

Antarctic Circle

**THE WORLD
IN 420 A.D.**

MAP 6

Roman Empire splits into Eastern and Western sections;
China divided; Ghana appears; Mayan States

Bantu - undefined area

© HAMMOND WORLD ATLAS CORPORATION

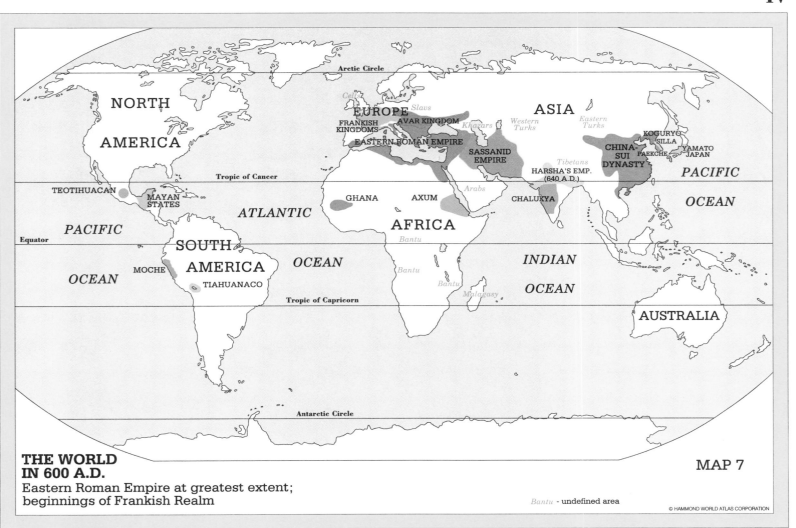

**THE WORLD
IN 600 A.D.**

Eastern Roman Empire at greatest extent;
beginnings of Frankish Realm

MAP 7

Bantu - undefined area

© HAMMOND WORLD ATLAS CORPORATION

Arctic Circle

Celts
Slavs
NORTH
AMERICA
EUROPE
AVAR KINGDOM
Khazars
Western Turks
Eastern Turks
ASIA
FRANKISH
KINGDOMS
EASTERN ROMAN EMPIRE
KOGURYO
SILLA
PAEKCHE
YAMATO
JAPAN
SASSANID
EMPIRE
CHINA-
SUI
DYNASTY
Tropic of Cancer
HARSHA'S EMP.
(640 A.D.)
PACIFIC
Arabs
Tibetans
TEOTIHUACAN
MAYAN
STATES
GHANA
AXUM
CHALUKYA
OCEAN
PACIFIC
ATLANTIC
AFRICA
Equator
SOUTH
AMERICA
Bantu
MOCHE
OCEAN
Bantu
INDIAN
TIAHUANACO
Bantu
OCEAN
OCEAN
Tropic of Capricorn
Malagasy
AUSTRALIA
Antarctic Circle

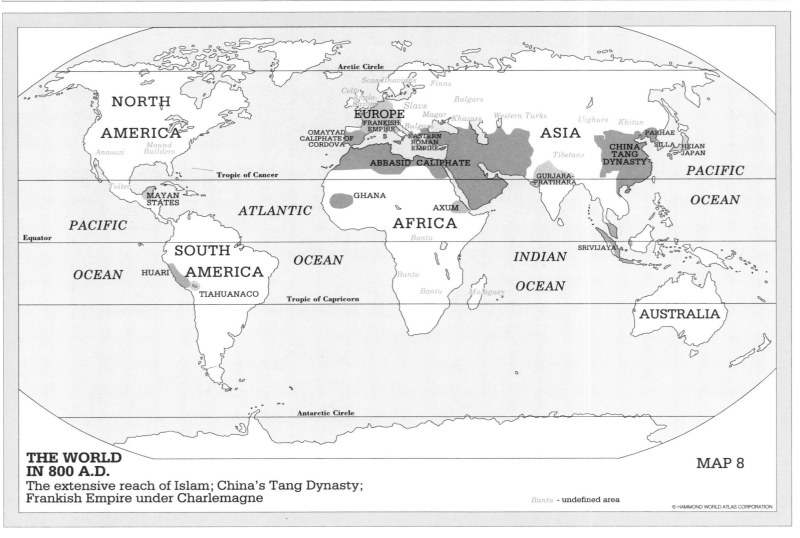

**THE WORLD
IN 800 A.D.**

The extensive reach of Islam; China's Tang Dynasty;
Frankish Empire under Charlemagne

MAP 8

Bantu - undefined area

© HAMMOND WORLD ATLAS CORPORATION

Arctic Circle

Scandinavians
Finns
NORTH
AMERICA
Celts
Anglo-Saxons
Slavs
Bulgars
Magar
Khazars
Western Turks
Uighurs
Khitan
EUROPE
FRANKISH
EMPIRE
Bulgars
ASIA
OMAYYAD
CALIPHATE OF
CORDOVA
EASTERN
ROMAN
EMPIRE
PARHAE
SILLA
HEIAN
JAPAN
Anasazi
*Mound
Builders*
ABBASID CALIPHATE
Tibetans
CHINA
TANG
DYNASTY
Tropic of Cancer
GURJARA-
PRATIHARA
PACIFIC
Toltec
MAYAN
STATES
GHANA
AXUM
OCEAN
PACIFIC
ATLANTIC
AFRICA
Equator
SOUTH
AMERICA
Bantu
SRIVIJAYA
OCEAN
HUARI
Bantu
INDIAN
TIAHUANACO
Bantu
OCEAN
OCEAN
Tropic of Capricorn
Malagasy
AUSTRALIA
Antarctic Circle

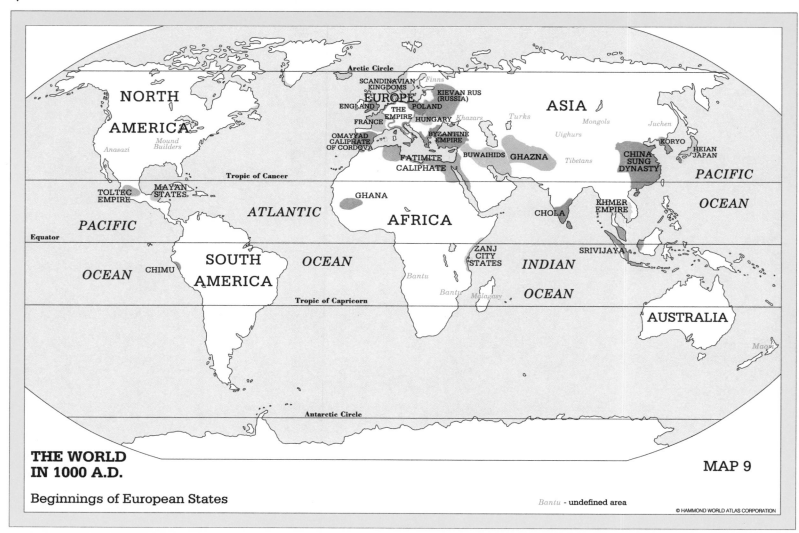

**THE WORLD
IN 1000 A.D.**

MAP 9

Beginnings of European States

Bantu - **undefined area**

© HAMMOND WORLD ATLAS CORPORATION

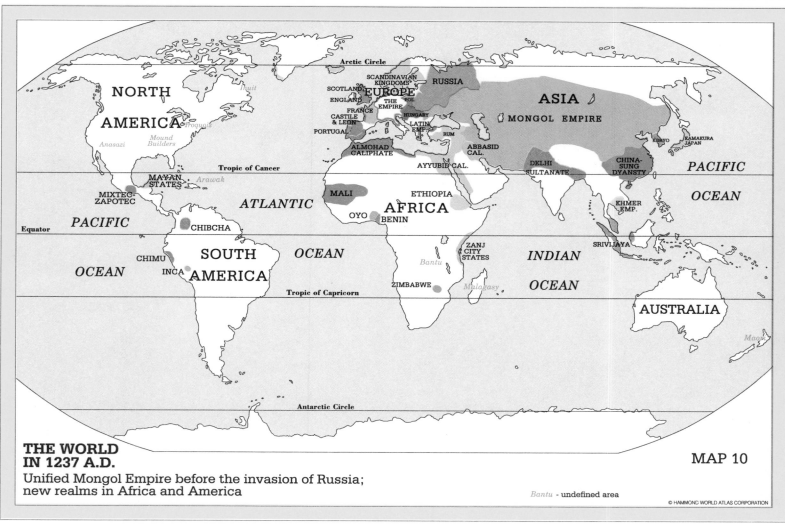

**THE WORLD
IN 1237 A.D.**

MAP 10

Unified Mongol Empire before the invasion of Russia;
new realms in Africa and America

Bantu - **undefined area**

© HAMMOND WORLD ATLAS CORPORATION

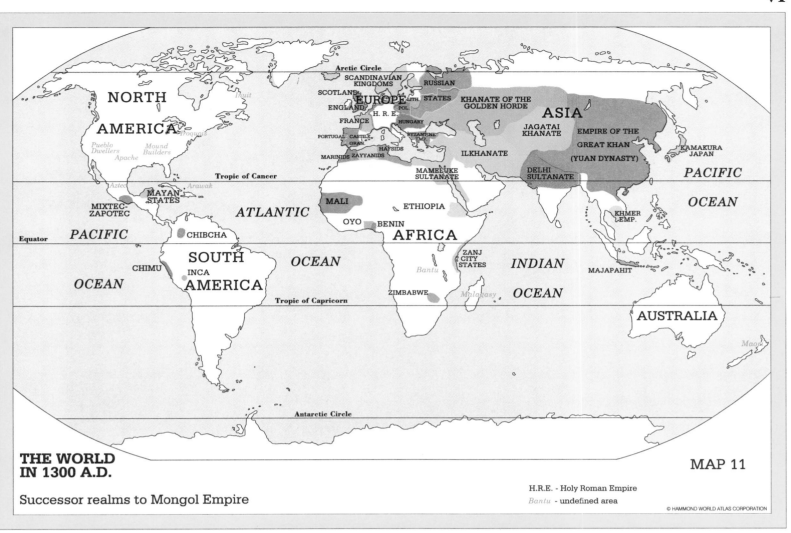

NORTH AMERICA

Inuit

Iroquois

Pueblo Dwellers *Mound Builders*

Apache

Aztec *Arawak*

MIXTEC-ZAPOTEC

MAYAN STATES

PACIFIC

OCEAN

CHIBCHA

CHIMU

INCA

SOUTH AMERICA

ATLANTIC

OCEAN

Arctic Circle

SCANDINAVIAN KINGDOMS

RUSSIAN STATES

SCOTLAND

EUROPE LITH.

ENGLAND POL.

H.R.E.

FRANCE HUNGARY

BYZANTINE EMP.

PORTUGAL CASTILE

GRAN.

MARINIDS ZAYYANIDS

HAFSIDS

KHANATE OF THE GOLDEN HORDE

ASIA

JAGATAI KHANATE

EMPIRE OF THE GREAT KHAN (YUAN DYNASTY)

ILKHANATE

KAMAKURA JAPAN

Tropic of Cancer

MAMELUKE SULTANATE

DELHI SULTANATE

PACIFIC

OCEAN

MALI

ETHIOPIA

OYO BENIN

KHMER EMP.

Equator

AFRICA

Bantu

ZANJ CITY STATES

INDIAN

MAJAPAHIT

ZIMBABWE *Malagasy*

OCEAN

Tropic of Capricorn

AUSTRALIA

Maori

Antarctic Circle

THE WORLD IN 1300 A.D.

Successor realms to Mongol Empire

MAP 11

H.R.E. - Holy Roman Empire

Bantu - undefined area

© HAMMOND WORLD ATLAS CORPORATION

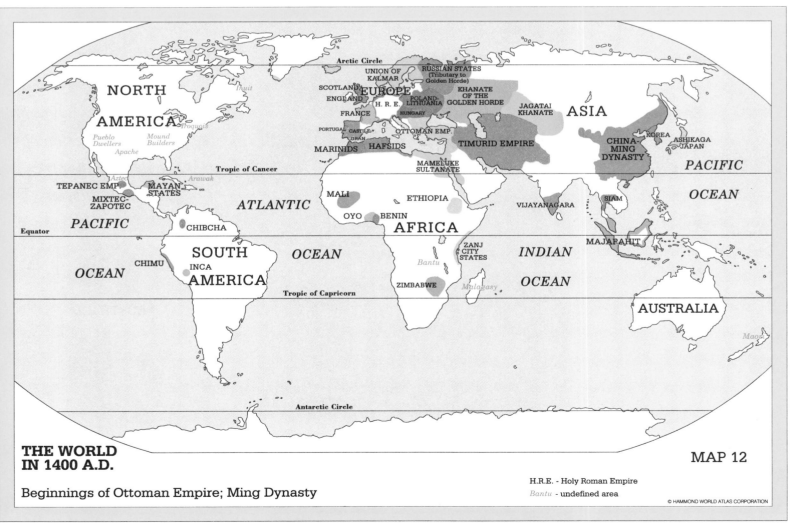

NORTH AMERICA

Inuit

Iroquois

Pueblo Dwellers *Mound Builders*

Apache

Aztec *Arawak*

TEPANEC EMP.

MIXTEC-ZAPOTEC

MAYAN STATES

PACIFIC

OCEAN

CHIBCHA

CHIMU

INCA

SOUTH AMERICA

ATLANTIC

OCEAN

Arctic Circle

UNION OF KALMAR

RUSSIAN STATES (Tributary to Golden Horde)

SCOTLAND

ENGLAND EUROPE

H.R.E.

FRANCE POLAND-LITHUANIA

HUNGARY

PORTUGAL CASTILE

GRAN.

MARINIDS HAFSIDS

OTTOMAN EMP.

KHANATE OF THE GOLDEN HORDE

JAGATAI KHANATE

ASIA

TIMURID EMPIRE

CHINA MING DYNASTY

KOREA

ASHIKAGA JAPAN

Tropic of Cancer

MAMELUKE SULTANATE

PACIFIC

OCEAN

MALI

ETHIOPIA

OYO BENIN

VIJAYANAGARA

SIAM

Equator

AFRICA

Bantu

ZANJ CITY STATES

INDIAN

MAJAPAHIT

ZIMBABWE *Malagasy*

OCEAN

Tropic of Capricorn

AUSTRALIA

Maori

Antarctic Circle

THE WORLD IN 1400 A.D.

Beginnings of Ottoman Empire; Ming Dynasty

MAP 12

H.R.E. - Holy Roman Empire

Bantu - undefined area

© HAMMOND WORLD ATLAS CORPORATION

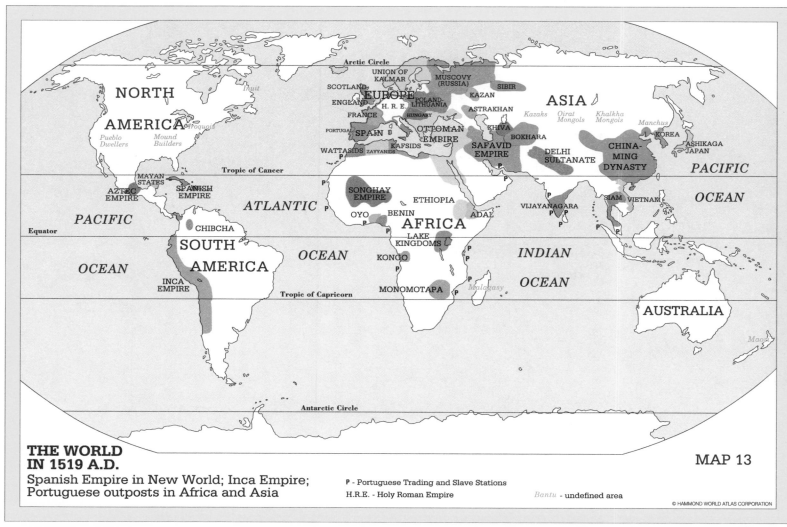

**THE WORLD
IN 1519 A.D.**

Spanish Empire in New World; Inca Empire;
Portuguese outposts in Africa and Asia

P - Portuguese Trading and Slave Stations

H.R.E. - Holy Roman Empire

Bantu - undefined area

MAP 13

© HAMMOND WORLD ATLAS CORPORATION

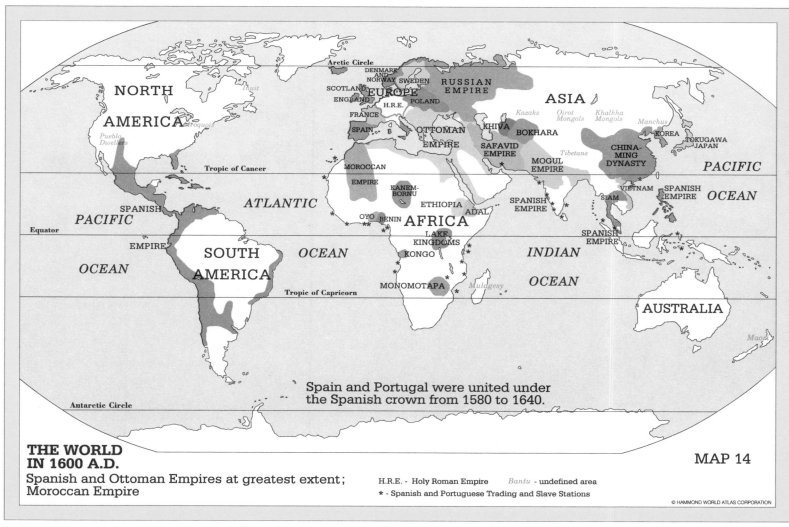

Spain and Portugal were united under
the Spanish crown from 1580 to 1640.

**THE WORLD
IN 1600 A.D.**

Spanish and Ottoman Empires at greatest extent;
Moroccan Empire

H.R.E. - Holy Roman Empire

Bantu - undefined area

* - Spanish and Portuguese Trading and Slave Stations

MAP 14

© HAMMOND WORLD ATLAS CORPORATION

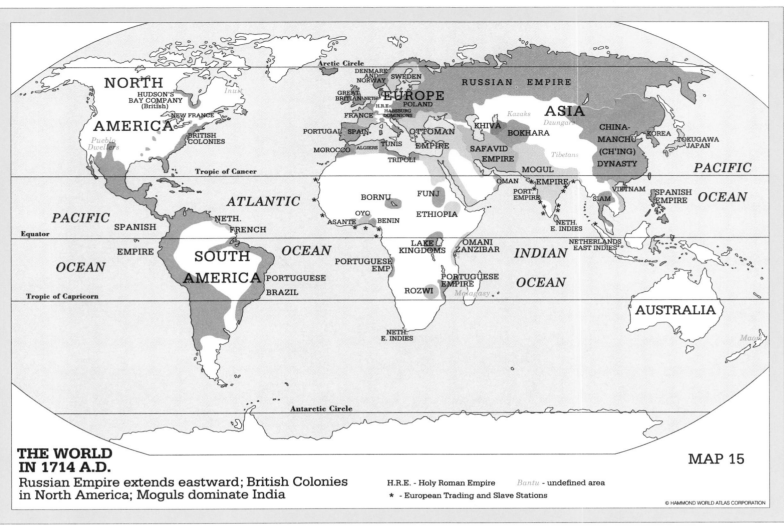

NORTH
AMERICA

HUDSON'S
BAY COMPANY
(British)

NEW FRANCE

BRITISH
COLONIES

*Pueblo
Dwellers*

ATLANTIC

NETH.
FRENCH

PACIFIC

SPANISH

Equator

EMPIRE

OCEAN

SOUTH
AMERICA

OCEAN

PORTUGUESE

BRAZIL

Tropic of Capricorn

Arctic Circle

DENMARK
AND
NORWAY   SWEDEN

RUSSIAN   EMPIRE

GREAT
BRITAIN NETH. EUROPE   POLAND

FRANCE   H.R.E.
HABSBURG
DOMINIONS

PORTUGAL SPAIN

MOROCCO   ALGIERS TUNIS

OTTOMAN

EMPIRE

TRIPOLI

Tropic of Cancer

Inuit

ASIA

Kazaks

KHIVA   *Dzungars*

BOKHARA

SAFAVID
EMPIRE

Tibetans

CHINA-
MANCHU
(CH'ING)
DYNASTY

KOREA

TOKUGAWA
JAPAN

PACIFIC

MOGUL

OMAN   * EMPIRE

PORT
EMPIRE

VIETNAM

SIAM

SPANISH
EMPIRE

OCEAN

BORNU   FUNJ

OYO   ETHIOPIA

ASANTE   BENIN

LAKE
KINGDOMS

NETH.
E. INDIES

OMANI
ZANZIBAR

NETHERLANDS
EAST INDIES

INDIAN

PORTUGUESE
EMP.

PORTUGUESE
EMPIRE

ROZWI   *Madagasy*

OCEAN

AUSTRALIA

Maori

NETH.
E. INDIES

Antarctic Circle

**THE WORLD
IN 1714 A.D.**

Russian Empire extends eastward; British Colonies
in North America; Moguls dominate India

H.R.E. - Holy Roman Empire   *Bantu* - undefined area

 * - European Trading and Slave Stations

MAP 15

© HAMMOND WORLD ATLAS CORPORATION

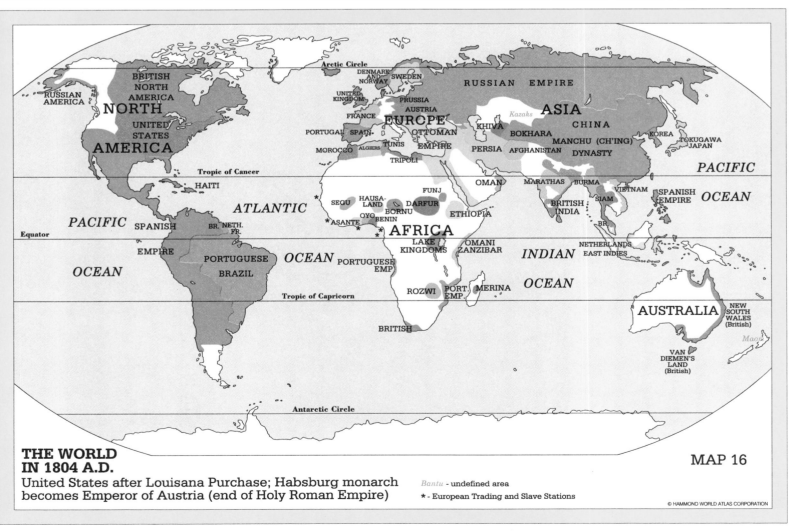

RUSSIAN
AMERICA

BRITISH
NORTH
AMERICA

NORTH
AMERICA

UNITED
STATES

HAITI

ATLANTIC

PACIFIC   SPANISH

Equator

EMPIRE

OCEAN

BR. NETH.
FR.

PORTUGUESE
BRAZIL

OCEAN

Tropic of Capricorn

Arctic Circle

DENMARK
AND
NORWAY   SWEDEN

RUSSIAN   EMPIRE

UNITED
KINGDOM   PRUSSIA
AUSTRIA

FRANCE   EUROPE

PORTUGAL SPAIN   OTTOMAN

MOROCCO   ALGIERS TUNIS   EMPIRE

TRIPOLI

Tropic of Cancer

ASIA

Kazaks

KHIVA

BOKHARA

PERSIA   AFGHANISTAN

CHINA

MANCHU (CH'ING)
DYNASTY

KOREA

TOKUGAWA
JAPAN

PACIFIC

OMAN   MARATHAS   BURMA

BRITISH
INDIA

VIETNAM
SIAM

BR.

SPANISH
EMPIRE

OCEAN

*   SEGU   HAUSA-
LAND   DARFUR   FUNJ

BORNU

OYO BENIN

* ASANTE   AFRICA

ETHIOPIA

LAKE
KINGDOMS

OMANI
ZANZIBAR

NETHERLANDS
EAST INDIES

INDIAN

PORTUGUESE
EMP.

ROZWI   PORT
EMP.   MERINA

OCEAN

AUSTRALIA

NEW
SOUTH
WALES
(British)

Maori

BRITISH

VAN
DIEMEN'S
LAND
(British)

Antarctic Circle

**THE WORLD
IN 1804 A.D.**

United States after Louisana Purchase; Habsburg monarch
becomes Emperor of Austria (end of Holy Roman Empire)

Bantu - undefined area

 * - European Trading and Slave Stations

MAP 16

© HAMMOND WORLD ATLAS CORPORATION

PREHISTORIC MAN

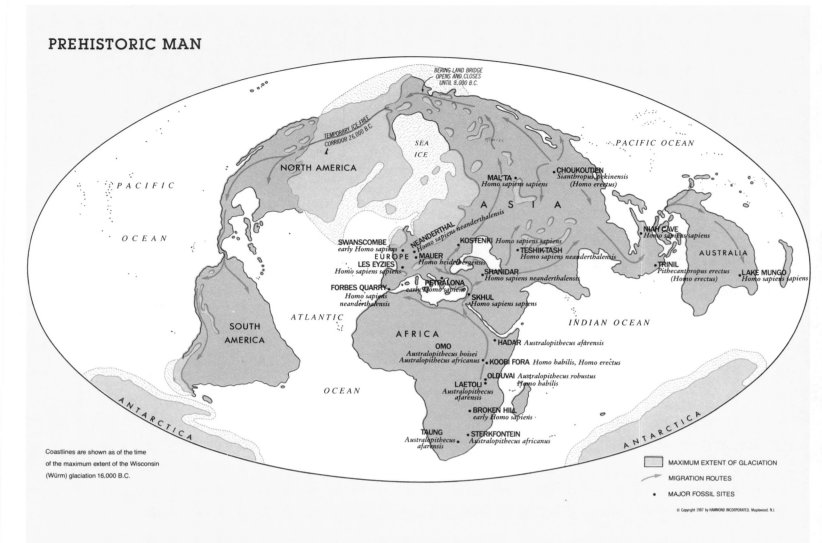

Coastlines are shown as of the time of the maximum extent of the Wisconsin (Würm) glaciation 16,000 B.C.

MAXIMUM EXTENT OF GLACIATION

MIGRATION ROUTES

MAJOR FOSSIL SITES

© Copyright 1987 by HAMMOND INCORPORATED, Maplewood, N.J.

THE SPREAD OF FARMING AND EARLY DOMESTICATION OF CROPS AND ANIMALS

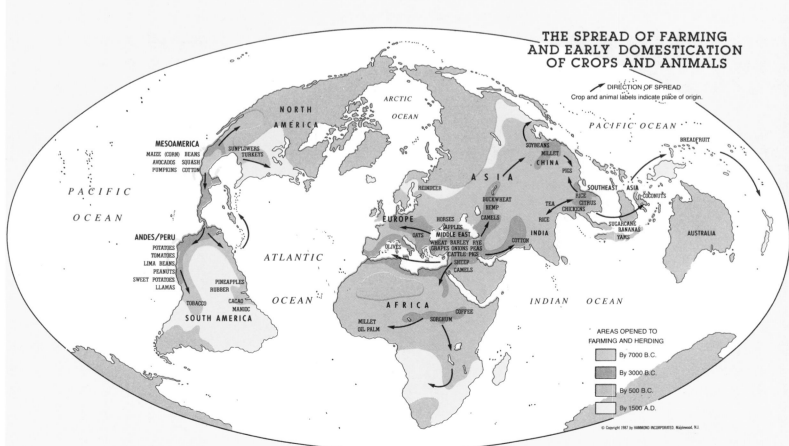

DIRECTION OF SPREAD
Crop and animal labels indicate place of origin.

AREAS OPENED TO FARMING AND HERDING

By 7000 B.C.
By 3000 B.C.
By 500 B.C.
By 1500 A.D.

© Copyright 1987 by HAMMOND INCORPORATED, Maplewood, N.J.

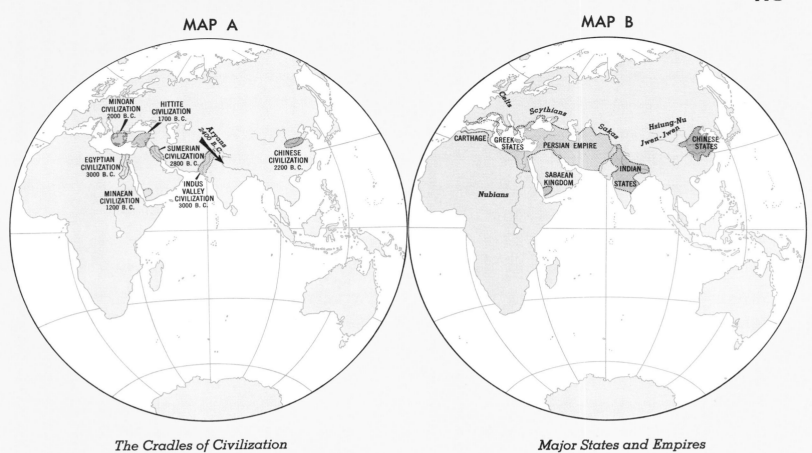

MAP A

The Cradles of Civilization
3000-1000 B.C.

MINOAN
CIVILIZATION
2000 B.C.

HITTITE
CIVILIZATION
1700 B.C.

Aryans
2400 B.C.

EGYPTIAN
CIVILIZATION
3000 B.C.

SUMERIAN
CIVILIZATION
2800 B.C.

CHINESE
CIVILIZATION
2200 B.C.

MINAEAN
CIVILIZATION
1200 B.C.

INDUS
VALLEY
CIVILIZATION
3000 B.C.

MAP B

Major States and Empires
in 500 B.C.

Celts

Scythians

Saka

Hsiung-Nu

Jwen-Jwen

CARTHAGE

GREEK
STATES

PERSIAN EMPIRE

CHINESE
STATES

Nubians

SABAEAN
KINGDOM

INDIAN
STATES

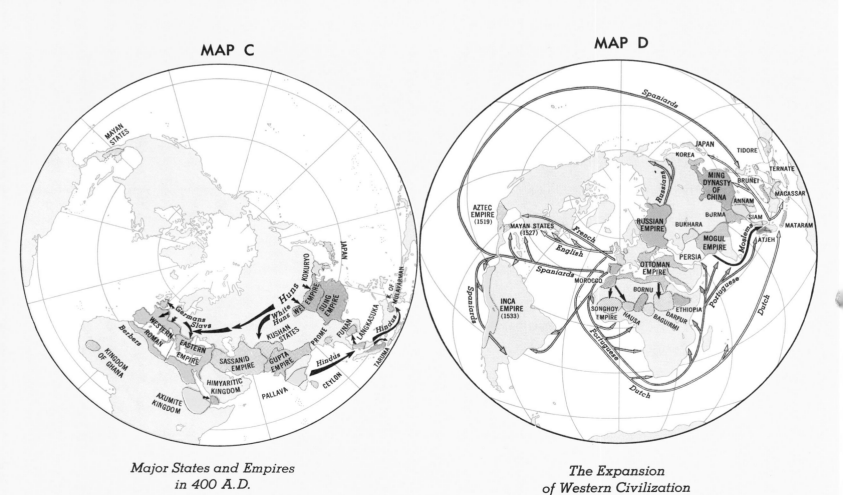

MAP C

Major States and Empires
in 400 A.D.

MAYAN
STATES

Huns

KOKURYO

JAPAN

White
Huns

W. EMPIRE

SUNG
EMPIRE

Germans

Slavs

WESTERN
ROMAN

K. OF
MULAVARMAN

Berbers

EASTERN
EMPIRE

KUSHAN
STATES

PROME

FUNAN

LANGKASUKA

Hindus

KINGDOM
OF GHANA

SASSANID
EMPIRE

GUPTA
EMPIRE

Hindus

TARUMA

HIMYARITIC
KINGDOM

PALLAVA

CEYLON

AXUMITE
KINGDOM

MAP D

The Expansion
of Western Civilization
1600 A.D.

Spaniards

JAPAN

TIDORE

KOREA

MING
DYNASTY
OF CHINA

BRUNEI

TERNATE

AZTEC
EMPIRE
(1519)

Russians

MACASSAR

MAYAN STATES
(1527)

French

RUSSIAN
EMPIRE

ANNAM

BURMA

SIAM

MATARAM

English

BUKHARA

MOGUL
EMPIRE

Moslems

ATJEH

Spaniards

PERSIA

Portuguese

INCA
EMPIRE
(1533)

Spaniards

OTTOMAN
EMPIRE

MOROCCO

Dutch

Spaniards

BORNU

SONGHOY
EMPIRE

HAUSA

DARFUR

ETHIOPIA

Portuguese

BAGUIRMI

Portuguese

Dutch

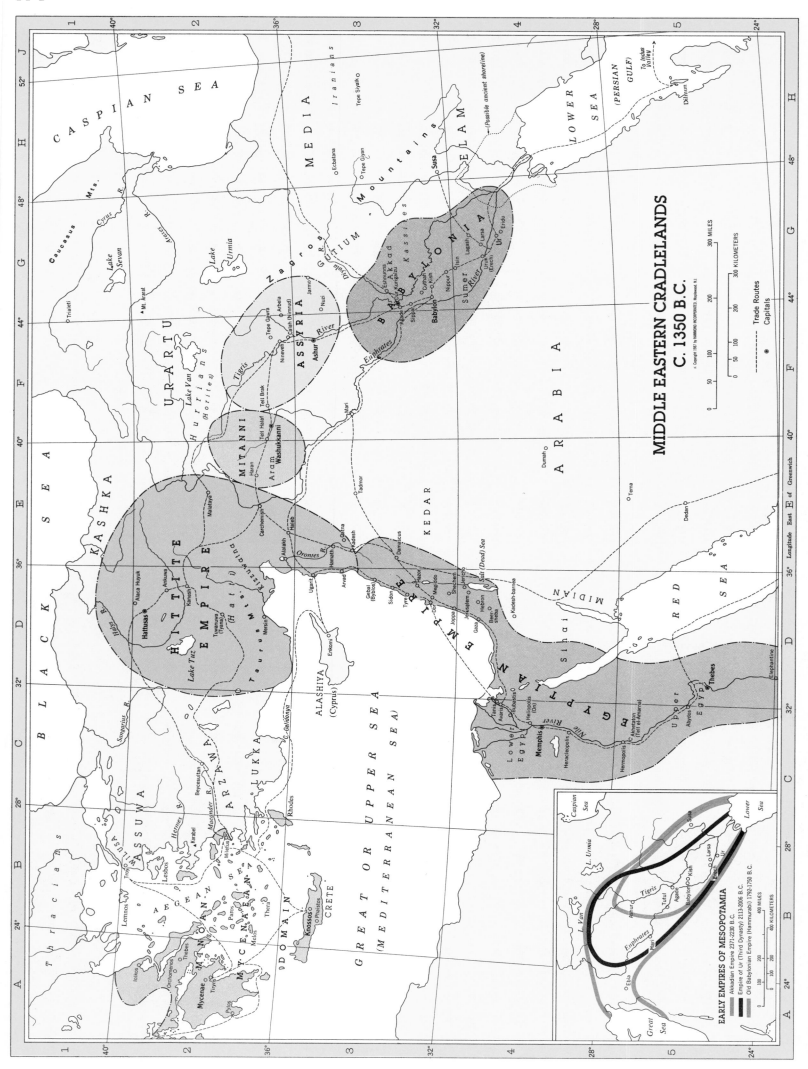

MIDDLE EASTERN CRADLELANDS
C. 1350 B.C.

© Copyright 1967 by HAMMOND INCORPORATED, Maplewood, N.J.

- - - - Trade Routes
● Capitals

300 MILES
300 KILOMETERS

EARLY EMPIRES OF MESOPOTAMIA

Akkadian Empire 2371-2230 B.C.
Empire of Ur (Third Dynasty) 2113-2006 B.C.
Old Babylonian Empire (Hammurabi) 1792-1750 B.C.

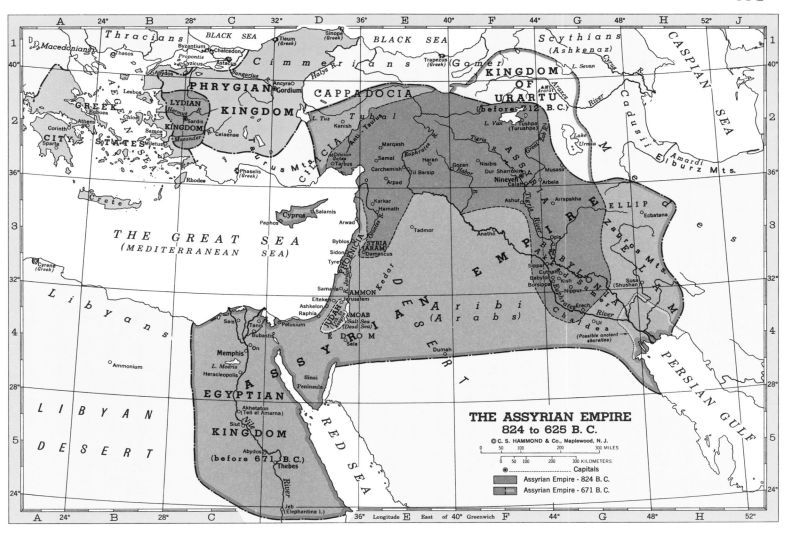

THE ASSYRIAN EMPIRE
824 to 625 B.C.

©C. S. HAMMOND & Co., Maplewood, N.J.

0	50	100	200	300 MILES

0	50	100	200	300 KILOMETERS

◉ ······ Capitals
Assyrian Empire - 824 B.C.
Assyrian Empire - 671 B.C.

GREAT EMPIRES OF THE
SIXTH CENTURY B.C.

©C. S. HAMMOND & Co., Maplewood, N.J

0	50	100	200	300	400	500 MILES

0	50	100	200	300	400	500 KILOMETERS

◉ Capitals
Limits of the Persian Empire c. 500 B. C.
Persian Royal Road
Red Sea - Nile Canal Built by Darius I

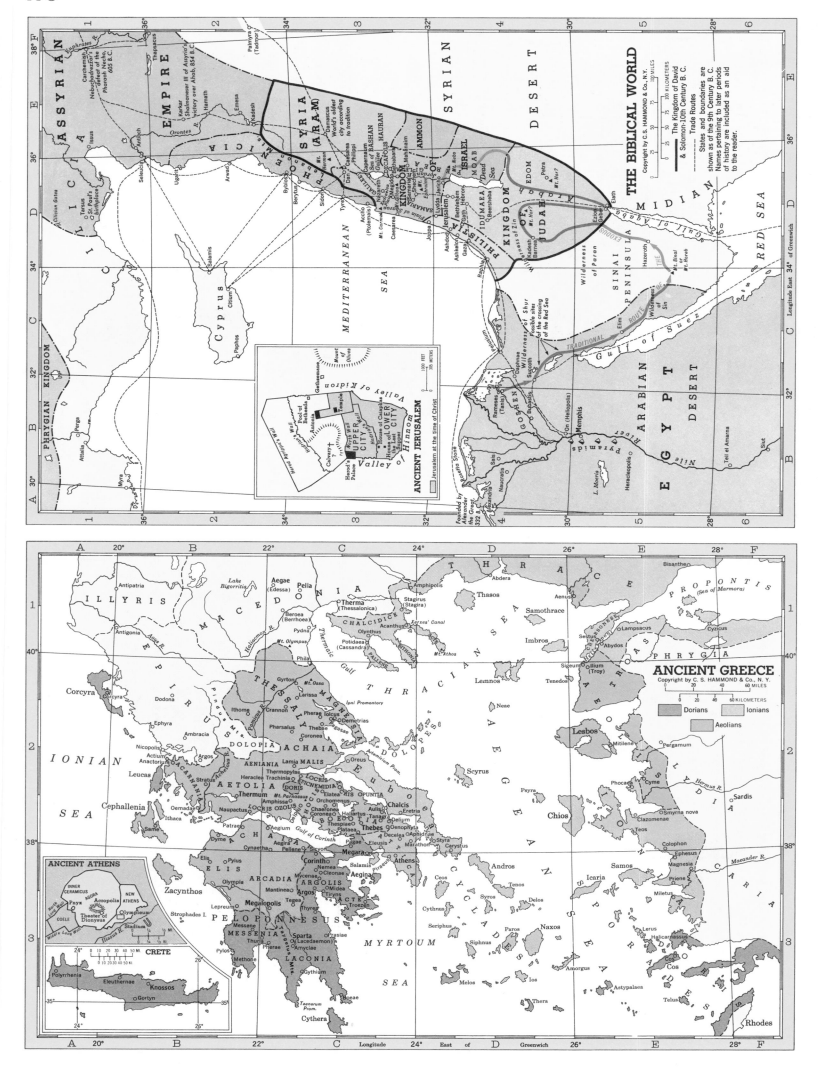

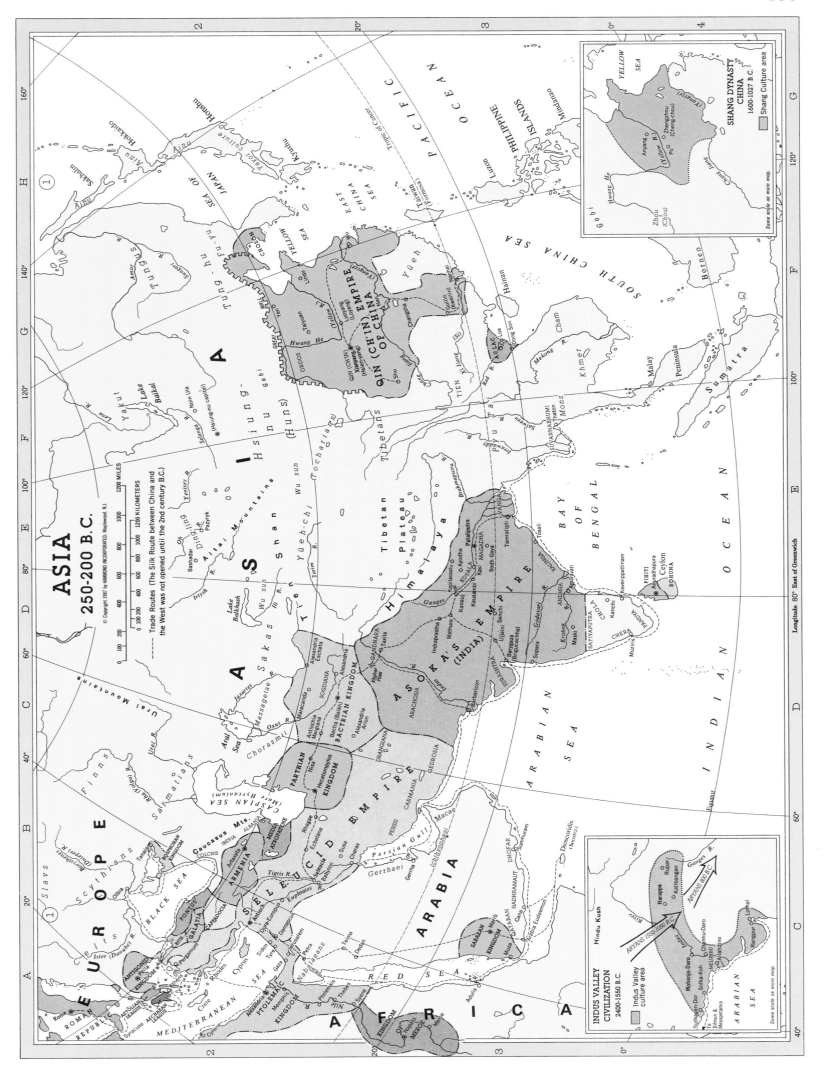

ASIA
250-200 B.C.

© Copyright 1987 by HAMMOND INCORPORATED, Maplewood, N.J.

—— Trade Routes (The Silk Route between China and
 the West was not opened until the 2nd century B.C.)

SHANG DYNASTY CHINA
1600-1027 B.C.

Shang Culture area

Same scale as main map.

INDUS VALLEY CIVILIZATION
2400-1550 B.C.

Indus Valley culture area

Same scale as main map.

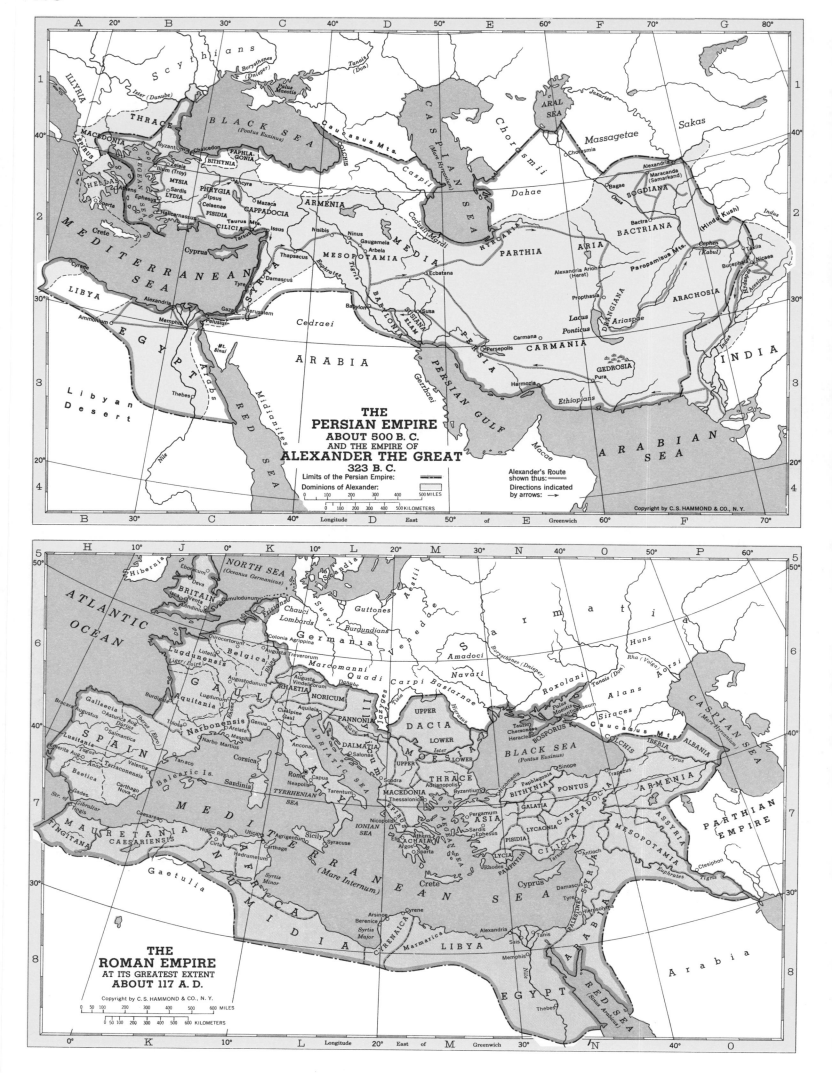

THE PERSIAN EMPIRE
ABOUT 500 B. C.
AND THE EMPIRE OF
ALEXANDER THE GREAT
323 B. C.

Limits of the Persian Empire:
Dominions of Alexander:

Alexander's Route shown thus:
Directions indicated by arrows:

Copyright by C. S. HAMMOND & CO., N.Y.

THE ROMAN EMPIRE
AT ITS GREATEST EXTENT
ABOUT 117 A. D.

Copyright by C. S. HAMMOND & CO., N. Y.

ANCIENT ITALY
ITALIA, LIGURIA, VENETIA, GALLIA-CISALPINA, HISTRIA, SICILIA & CORSICA
Before the time of Augustus

Copyright by C.S. HAMMOND & CO., N.Y.

0   20   40   60   80   100 MILES
0 20 40 60 80 100 KILOMETERS

Roman Colonies, thus; ———— **Ostia**
Greek Colonies, thus; ---- **SYRACUSAE (G)**
Carthaginian Colonies, thus; ---- **Eryx (C)**
Dotted lines show the Modern shore line

THE FORUM CAPITOLIUM and PALATIUM
1. Templum Saturni
2. Templum Concordiae
3. Scalae Gemoniae
4. Carcer (Tullianum)
5. Senaculum
6. Graecostasis
7. Rostra
8. Templum Jani

IMPERIAL FORA
1. Scalae Gemoniae
2. Templum Vespasiani
3. Porticus Deorum Consentium
4. Equus Caesaris
5. T. Castoris et Pollucis
6. Templum Divi Julii
7. Arcus Augusti
8. Arcus Titi
9. Templum Antonini et Faustinae

ROME
Under the Emperors

1. Templum Jovis Capitolini
2. Arx
3. Forum Romanum
4. Templum Aesculapii
5. Forum Trajani
6. Forum Augusti
7. Porta Carmentalis
8. Arcus Septimii Severi
9. Arcus Constantini
10. Arcus Titi
11. Arcus Claudii
12. Arcus Tiberii
13. Arcus Gallieni
14. Arcus Marci Aurelii
15. Arcus Diocletiani
16. Porta Flumentara
17. Templum Mercurji
18. Theatrum Marcelli

REGIONES AUGUSTI
I. Porta Capena
II. Caelimontium
III. Isis et Serapis
IV. Templum Pacis
V. Esquiliae
VI. Alta Semita
VII. Via Lata
VIII. Forum Romanum
IX. Circus Flaminius
X. Palatium
XI. Circus Maximus
XII. Piscina Publica
XIII. Aventinus
XIV. Trans Tiberim

ROME
In the time of the Republic

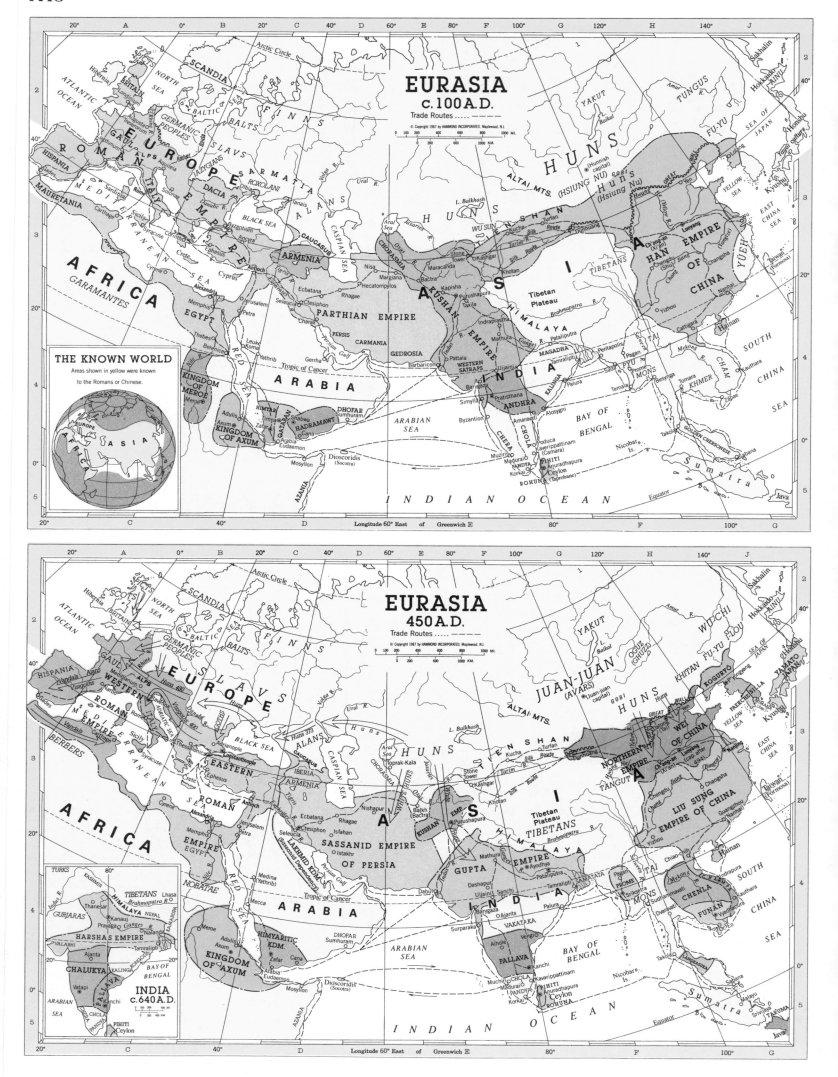

EURASIA
c. 100 A.D.
Trade Routes .....

© Copyright 1987 by HAMMOND INCORPORATED, Maplewood, N.J.

THE KNOWN WORLD
Areas shown in yellow were known to the Romans or Chinese.

Longitude 60° East of Greenwich E

EURASIA
450 A.D.
Trade Routes .....

© Copyright 1987 by HAMMOND INCORPORATED, Maplewood, N.J.

INDIA c. 640 A.D.

Longitude 60° East of Greenwich E

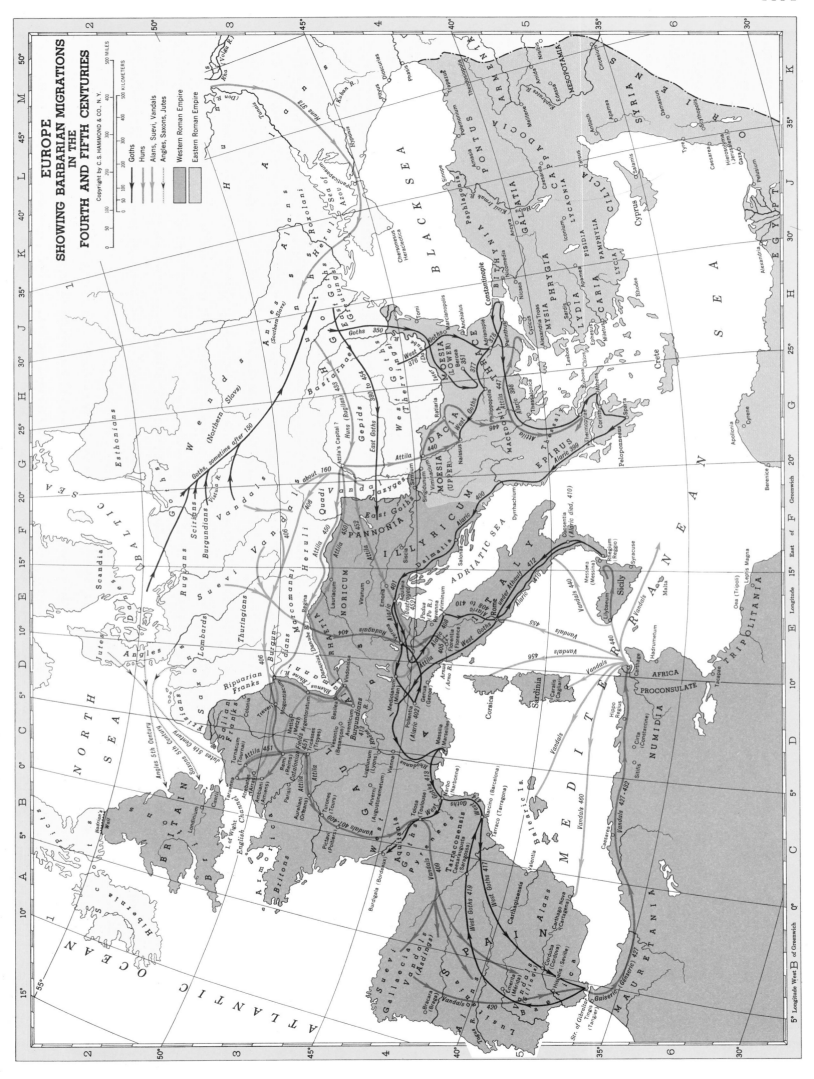

EUROPE
SHOWING BARBARIAN MIGRATIONS
IN THE
FOURTH AND FIFTH CENTURIES

Copyright by C.S. HAMMOND & CO., N.Y.

Goths
Huns
Alans, Suevi, Vandals
Angles, Saxons, Jutes
Western Roman Empire
Eastern Roman Empire

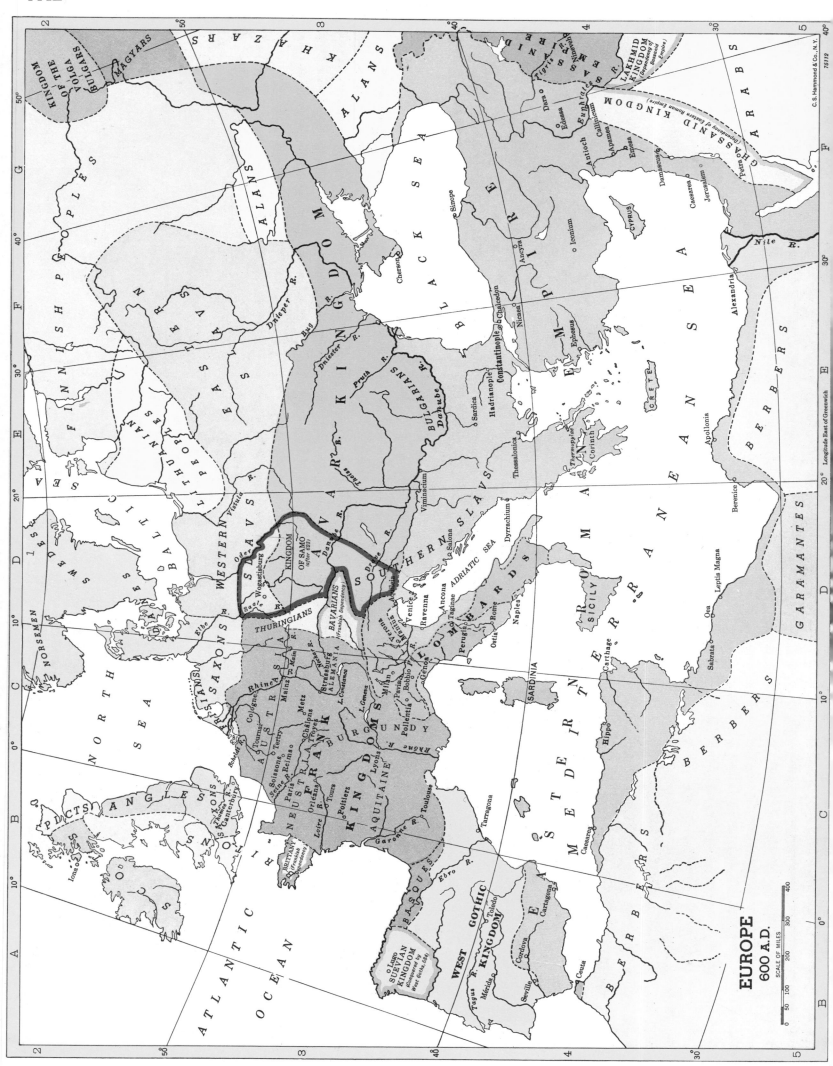

EUROPE
600 A.D.

SCALE OF MILES

0 50 100   200   300   400

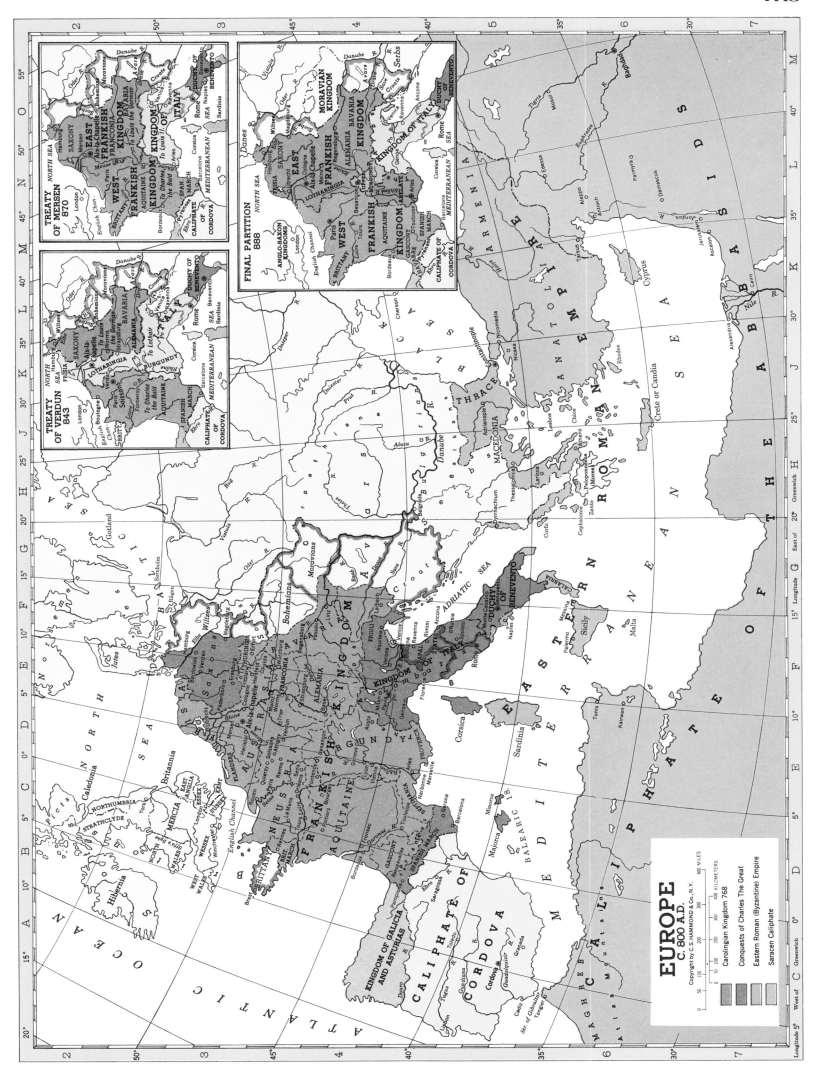

EUROPE
C. 800 A.D.

Copyright by C. S. Hammond & Co., N.Y.

Carolingian Kingdom 768
Conquests of Charles The Great
Eastern Roman (Byzantine) Empire
Saracen Caliphate

TREATY OF MERSEN 870

TREATY OF VERDUN 843

FINAL PARTITION 888

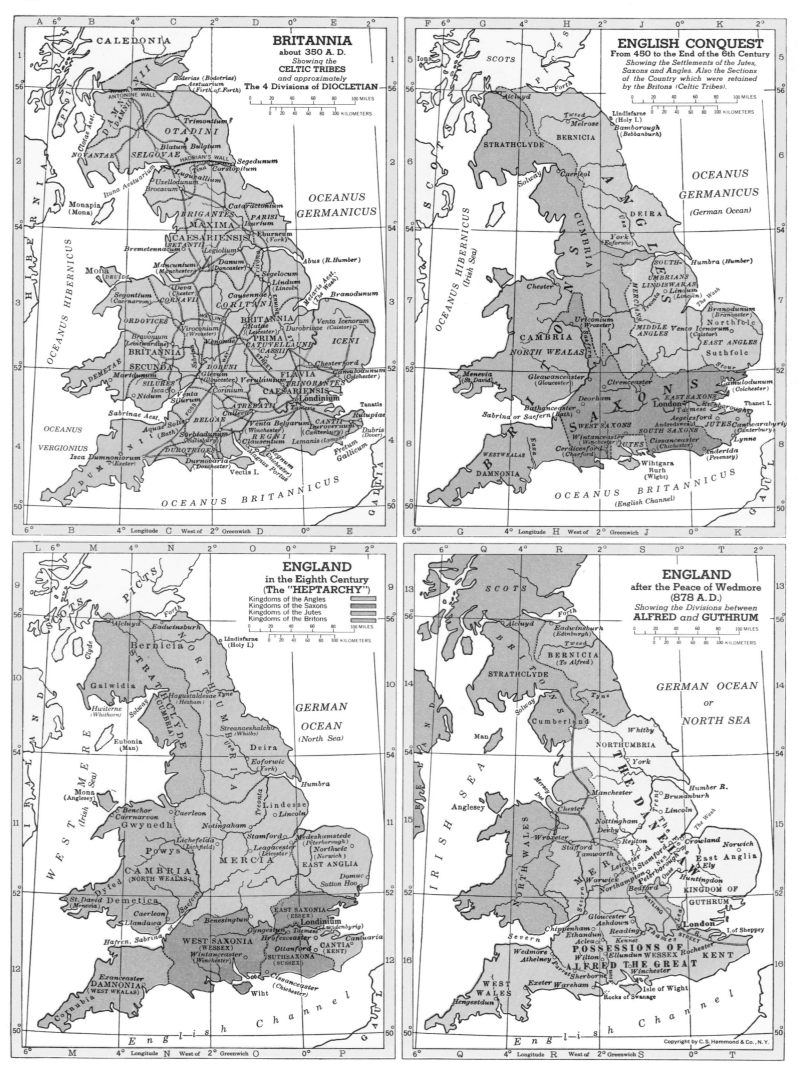

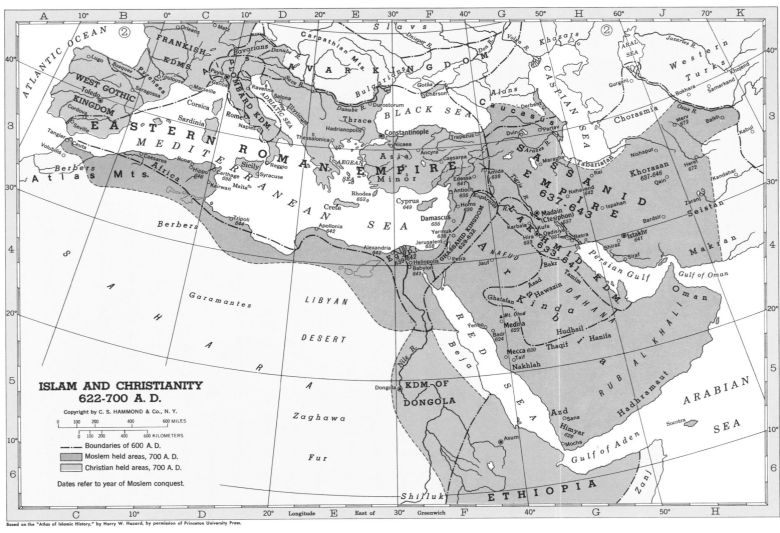

ISLAM AND CHRISTIANITY
622-700 A.D.

Copyright by C. S. Hammond & Co., N. Y.

Boundaries of 600 A. D.
Moslem held areas, 700 A. D.
Christian held areas, 700 A. D.

Dates refer to year of Moslem conquest.

Based on the "Atlas of Islamic History," by Harry W. Hazard, by permission of Princeton University Press.

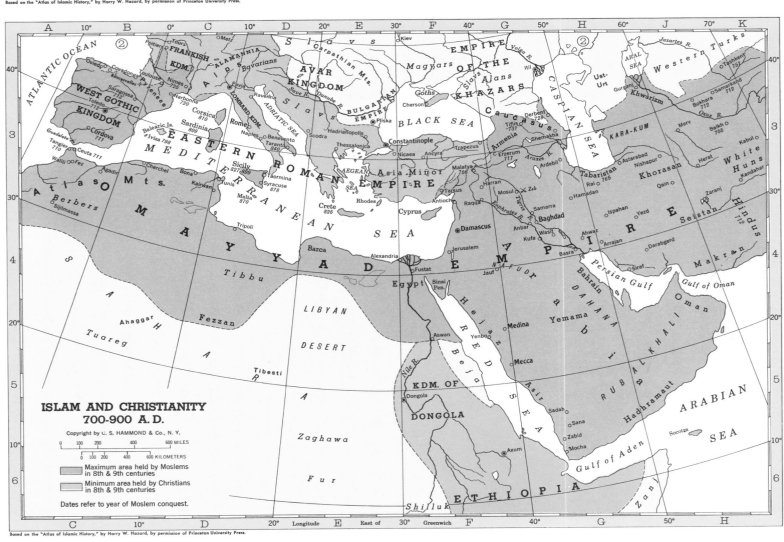

ISLAM AND CHRISTIANITY
700-900 A.D.

Copyright by C. S. Hammond & Co., N. Y.

Maximum area held by Moslems in 8th & 9th centuries
Minimum area held by Christians in 8th & 9th centuries

Dates refer to year of Moslem conquest.

Based on the "Atlas of Islamic History," by Harry W. Hazard, by permission of Princeton University Press.

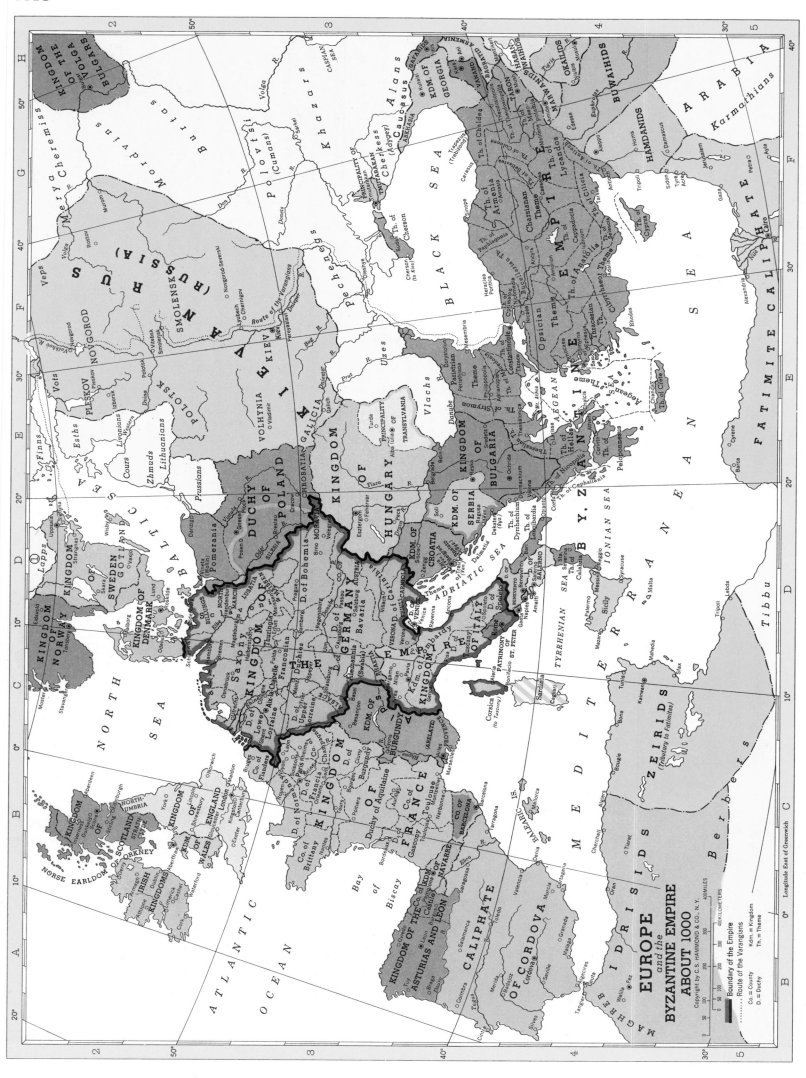

EUROPE
and the
BYZANTINE EMPIRE
ABOUT 1000

Copyright by C.S. Hammond & Co., N.Y.

Boundary of the Empire
Route of the Varangians

Co. = County   Kdm. = Kingdom
D. = Duchy   Th. = Theme

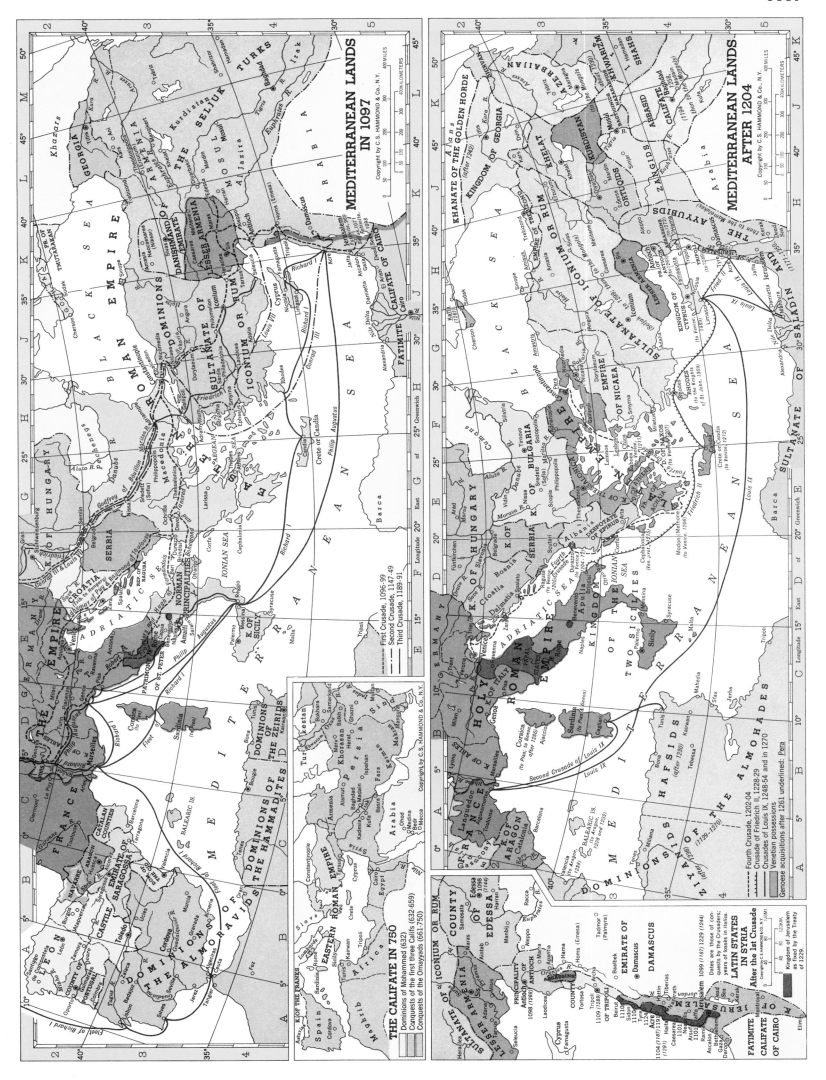

MEDITERRANEAN LANDS IN 1097

Copyright by C.S. HAMMOND & Co., N.Y.

First Crusade, 1096-99
Second Crusade, 1147-49
Third Crusade, 1189-91

THE CALIFATE IN 750

Dominions of Mohammed (632)
Conquests of the first three Califs (632-659)
Conquests of the Omayyads (661-750)

Copyright by C.S. HAMMOND & Co., N.Y.

MEDITERRANEAN LANDS AFTER 1204

Copyright by C.S. HAMMOND & Co., N.Y.

Fourth Crusade, 1202-04
Crusade of Friedrich II, 1228-29
Crusades of Louis IX, 1248-54 and in 1270
Venetian possessions
Genoese acquisitions after 1261 underlined: Pera

LATIN STATES IN SYRIA After the 1st Crusade

Dates are those of conquests by the Crusaders; years of losses in *italics*.

Kingdom of Jerusalem as fixed by the Treaty of 1229.

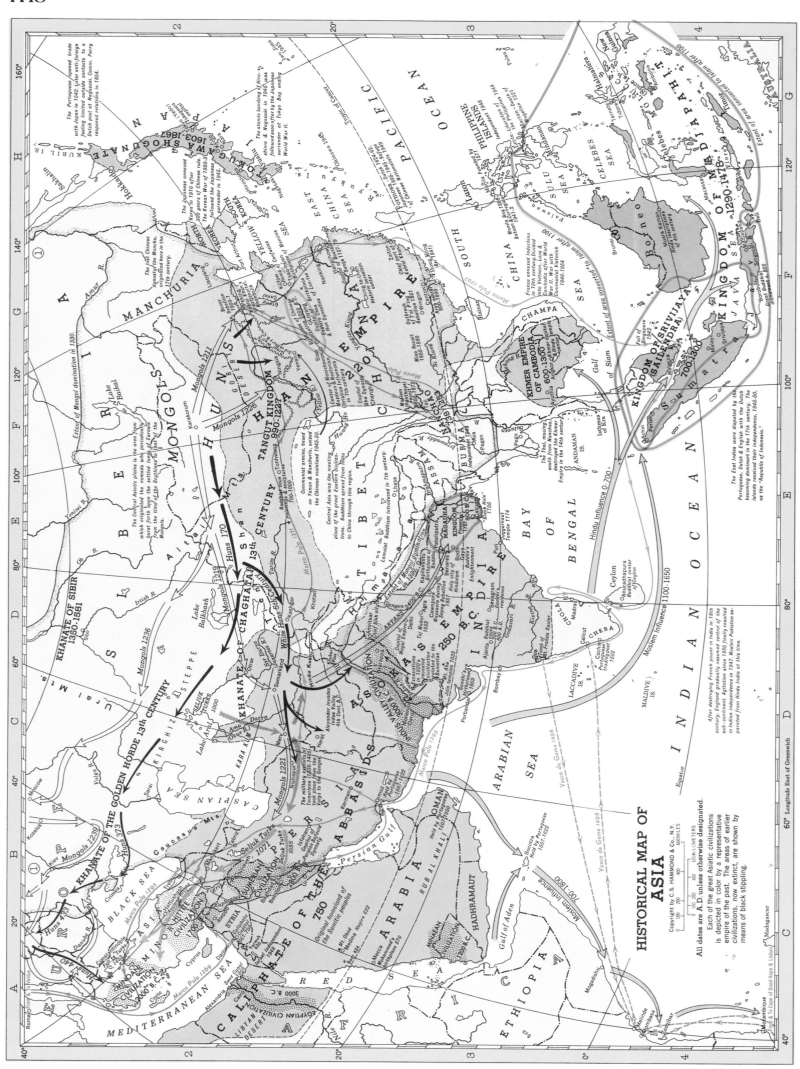

HISTORICAL MAP OF ASIA

Copyright by C.S. Hammond & Co., N.Y.

Each of the great Asiatic civilizations is depicted in color by a representative empire of the past. The areas of earlier civilizations, now extinct, are shown by means of black stippling.

All dates are A.D. unless otherwise designated.

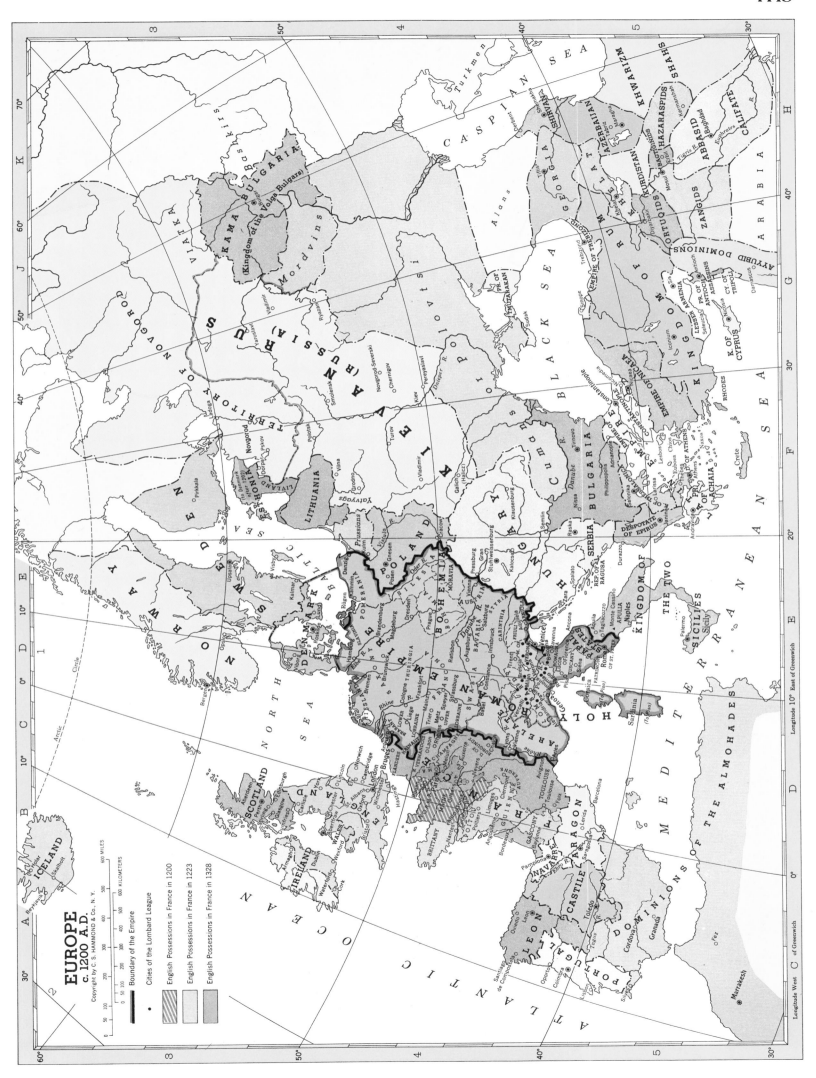

EUROPE
c. 1200 A.D.

Copyright by C. S. HAMMOND & Co., N.Y.

Boundary of the Empire
· Cities of the Lombard League
English Possessions in France in 1200
English Possessions in France in 1223
English Possessions in France in 1328

MILES
KILOMETERS

ECCLESIASTICAL MAP OF
EUROPE
c. 1300 A. D.

GREENLAND
Gardar
(To Trondjem)
Same scale as main map

Archbishoprics
Bishoprics
Monasteries
Universities
The Archepiscopal provinces are colored

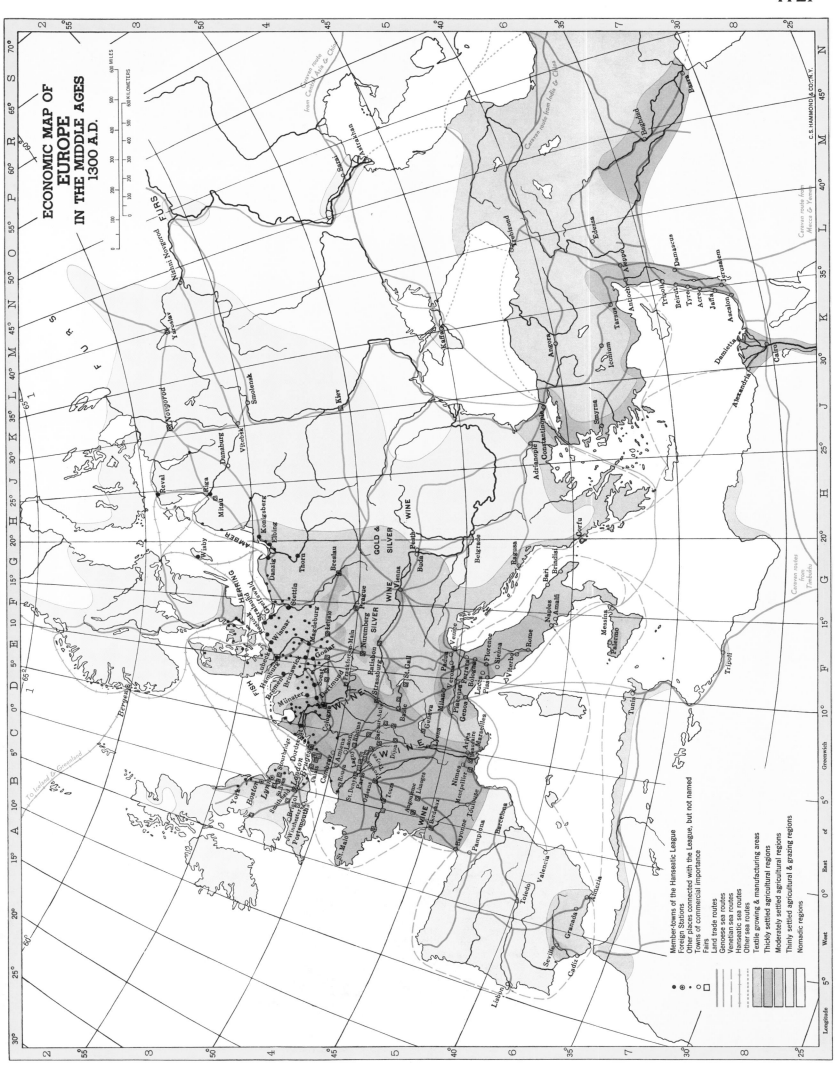

ECONOMIC MAP OF
EUROPE
IN THE MIDDLE AGES
1300 A.D.

Member-towns of the Hanseatic League
Foreign Stations
Other places connected with the League, but not named
Towns of commercial importance
Fairs
Land trade routes
Genoese sea routes
Venetian sea routes
Hanseatic sea routes
Other sea routes
Textile growing & manufacturing areas
Thickly settled agricultural regions
Moderately settled agricultural regions
Thinly settled agricultural & grazing regions
Nomadic regions

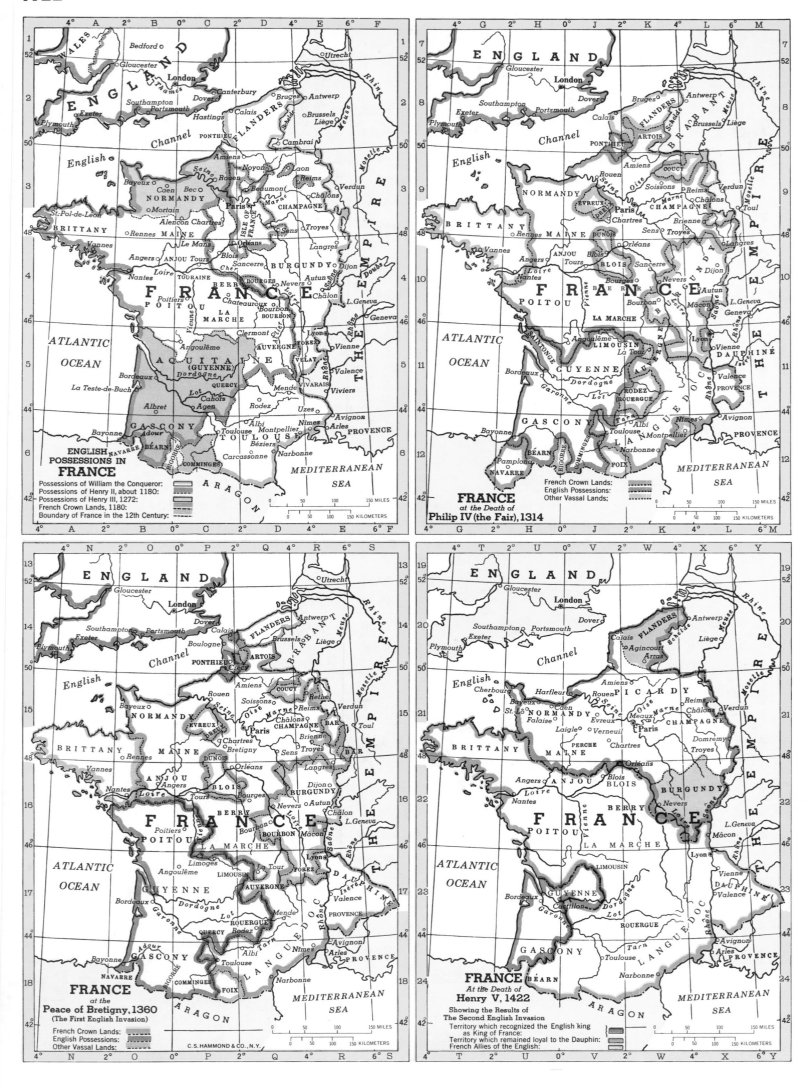

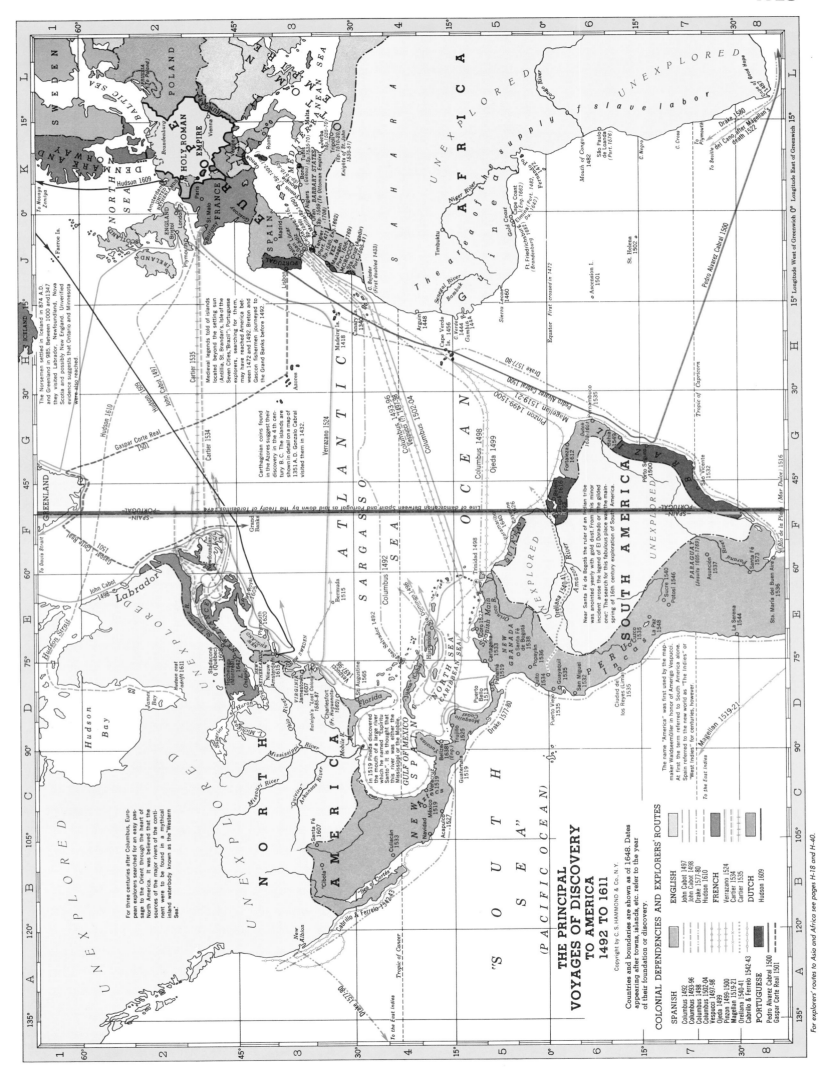

THE PRINCIPAL VOYAGES OF DISCOVERY TO AMERICA 1492 TO 1611

Copyright by C. S. HAMMOND & Co., N.Y.

Countries and boundaries are shown as of 1648. Dates appearing after towns, islands, etc. refer to the year of their foundation or discovery.

COLONIAL DEPENDENCIES AND EXPLORERS' ROUTES

SPANISH
Columbus 1492
Columbus 1493-96
Columbus 1498
Columbus 1502-04
Vespucci 1497-98
Ojeda 1499
Pinzon 1499-1500
Magellan 1519-21
Orellana 1540-41
Cabrillo & Ferrelo 1542-43

ENGLISH
John Cabot 1497
John Cabot 1498
Drake 1577-80
Hudson 1610

FRENCH
Verrazano 1524
Cartier 1534
Cartier 1535

DUTCH
Hudson 1609

PORTUGUESE
Pedro Alvarez Cabral 1500
Gaspar Corte Real 1501

For three centuries after Columbus, European explorers searched for an easy passage to the Orient through the heart of North America. It was believed that the sources of the major rivers of the continent were to be found in a mythical inland waterbody known as the "Western Sea".

The Norsemen settled in Iceland in 874 A.D. and Greenland in 985. Between 1000 and 1347 they visited Labrador, Newfoundland, Nova Scotia and possibly New England. Unverified evidence suggests that Ontario and Minnesota were also reached.

Medieval legends told of islands located beyond the setting sun (Antilia, St. Brandan's, Isle of the Seven Cities, "Brazil"). Portuguese explorers, searching for them, may have reached America between 1472 and 1492. Breton and Gascon fishermen journeyed to the Grand Banks before 1492.

Carthaginian coins found in the Azores suggest their discovery in the 4th century B.C. The islands are shown in detail on a map of 1351 A.D. Gonzalo Cabral visited them in 1432.

In 1519 Pineda discovered the mouth of a large river which he named "Espiritu Santo". It is thought that this river was either the Mississippi or the Mobile.

Near Santa Fé de Bogotá the ruler of an Indian tribe was anointed yearly with gold dust. From this minor incident arose the legend of El Dorado or the gilded one". The search for this fabulous place was the mainspring of 16th century exploration of South America.

The name "America" was first used by the mapmaker Waldseemüller in honor of Amerigo Vespucci. At first the term referred to South America alone. Spain referred to the new world as "The Indies" or "West Indies" for centuries, however.

For explorers' routes to Asia and Africa see pages H-18 and H-40.

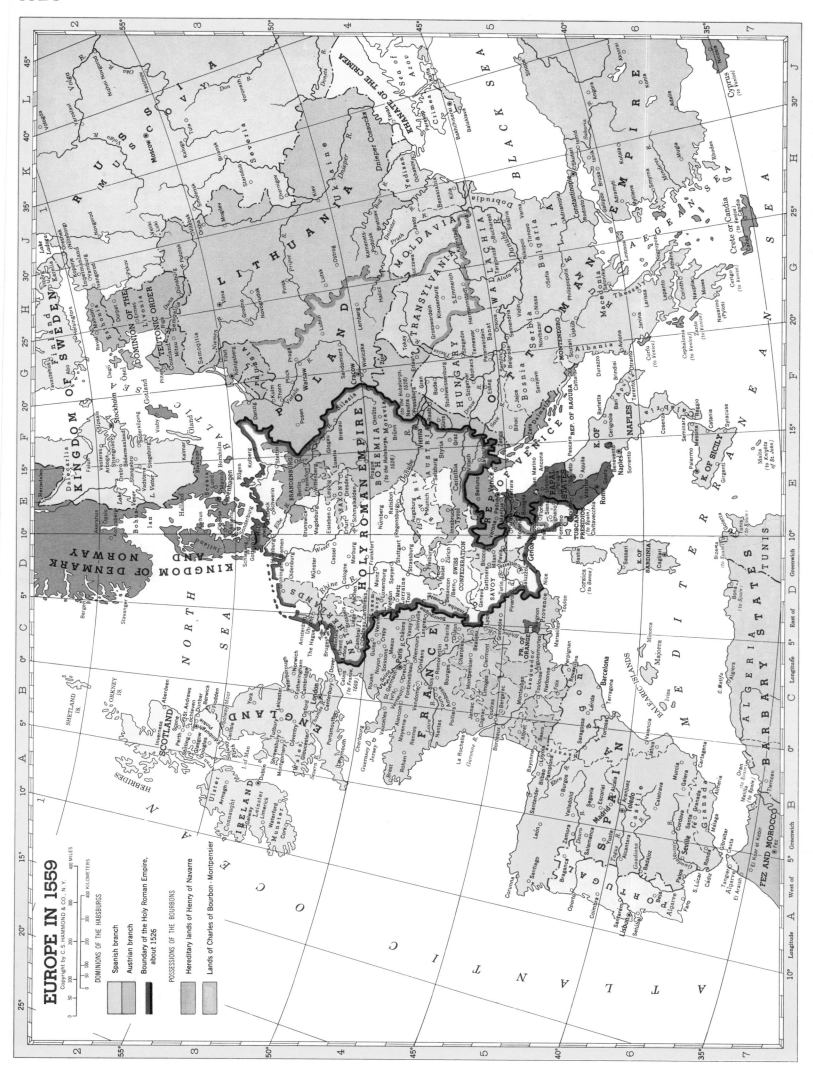

EUROPE IN 1559

Copyright by C. S. HAMMOND & CO., N.Y.

DOMINIONS OF THE HABSBURGS

Spanish branch

Austrian branch

Boundary of the Holy Roman Empire, about 1526

POSSESSIONS OF THE BOURBONS

Hereditary lands of Henry of Navarre

Lands of Charles of Bourbon-Montpensier

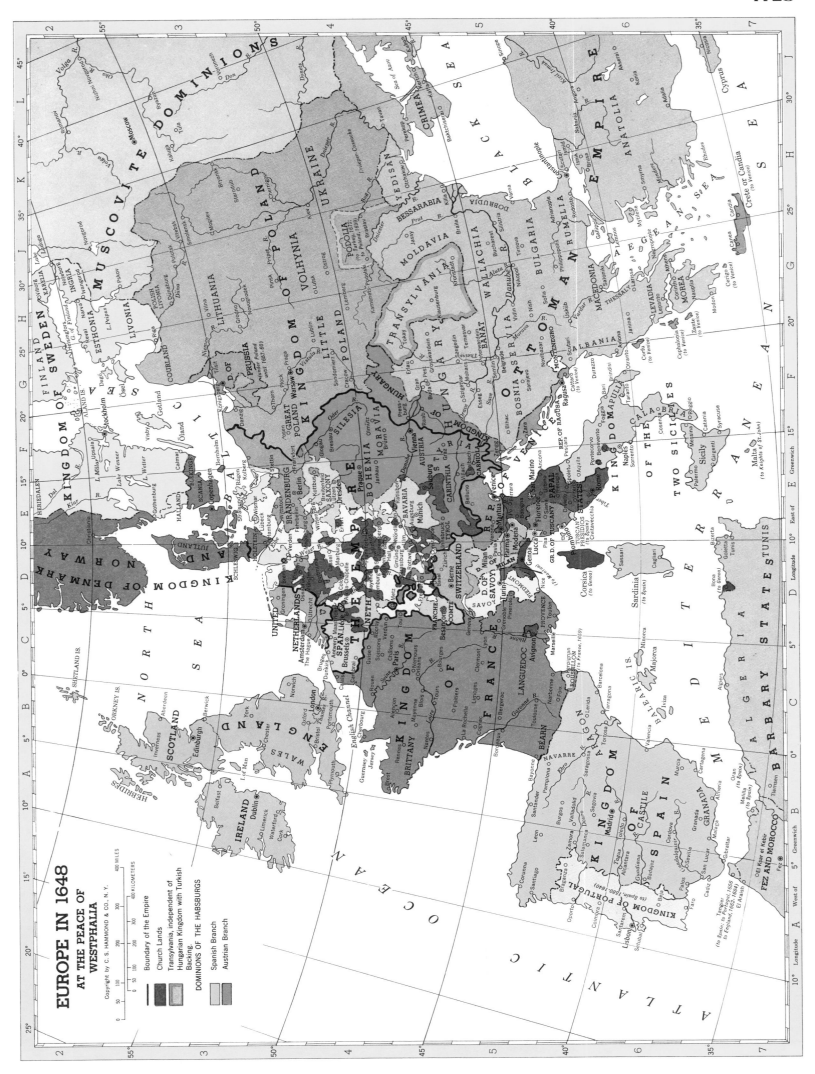

EUROPE IN 1648
AT THE PEACE OF WESTPHALIA

Copyright by C. S. HAMMOND & CO., N.Y.

400 MILES
400 KILOMETERS

Boundary of the Empire

Church Lands

Transylvania, independent of
Hungarian Kingdom with Turkish
Backing.

DOMINIONS OF THE HABSBURGS

Spanish Branch

Austrian Branch

EUROPE IN 1713-1714
AT THE TREATIES OF UTRECHT AND RASTATT
Copyright by C. S. HAMMOND & CO., N.Y.

Boundary of the Empire

Habsburg Dominions

Dominions of the Spanish Bourbons

Kingdom of Prussia

Church Lands

SHETLAND IS.

ORKNEY IS.

KINGDOM OF DENMARK AND NORWAY

KINGDOM OF SWEDEN

FINLAND

RUSSIAN EMPIRE

Moscow

HEBRIDES

KINGDOM OF NORTH SEA

Christiania

Gothenburg

Stockholm

ALAND IS.

Gulf of Finland

Helsingfors

St. Petersburg

INGRIA

L. Ladoga

Novgorod

ESTONIA (to Russia, 1721)

L. Peipus

LIVONIA

KINGDOM OF GREAT BRITAIN AND IRELAND

Edinburgh

Belfast

Dublin

Liverpool

Copenhagen

Rügen

Bornholm

Königsberg

Danzig

COURLAND

POLISH LIVONIA

Duna R.

Niemen R.

Vilna

LITHUANIA

Gotland

Öland

L. Wenner

L. Wetter

L. Malar

Riga

Plymouth

Portsmouth

London

Amsterdam

Ryswick

UNITED NETHERLANDS

Utrecht

Hamburg

Bremen

Verden

Stettin

DUCHY OF PRUSSIA (to Prussia, 1720)

GREAT POLAND

KINGDOM OF POLAND

Warsaw

VOLHYNIA

Pripet R.

Kiev

UKRAINE

Donets R.

English Channel

Boulogne

Amiens

Oudenarde

Ramillies

Brussels

AUSTR. NETH.

Cologne

Hanover

HANOVER

Berlin

SAXONY

Dresden

SILESIA

Vistula R.

LITTLE POLAND

PODOLIA

Bug R.

YEDISAN

Dnieper R.

Sea of Azov

BRITTANY

Brest

Rennes

Nantes

Versailles

Paris

Rouen

Fontenoy

Malplaquet

Metz

LORRAINE

Blenheim

Strassburg

Rastatt

Mainz

Frankfort

THE EMPIRE

BOHEMIA

Prague

MORAVIA

AUSTRIA

Vienna

Pressburg

Buda

Pest

KINGDOM OF HUNGARY

TRANSYLVANIA

MOLDAVIA

BESSARABIA

CRIMEA

BLACK SEA

KINGDOM OF FRANCE

Orléans

Loire R.

Lyons

Geneva

Berne

SWITZERLAND

Zürich

BAVARIA

Munich

TYROL

CARINTHIA

CARNIOLA

Agram R.

Drave R.

Save R.

BANAT (to Austria, 1718)

Theiss R.

LITTLE WALLACHIA

GREAT WALLACHIA

Bucharest

DOBRUDJA

Rochefort

Bordeaux

Montauban

Avignon

Nîmes

Marseilles

Toulon

Garonne R.

Bayonne

Toulouse

SAVOY

Turin

Milan

Parma

Modena

Venice

Trieste

REP. OF VENICE

BOSNIA

Belgrade

SERVIA

Danube R.

HERZE-GOVINA

MONTENEGRO

Cattaro

Sofia

BULGARIA

RUMELIA

Adrianople

Constantinople

ANATOLIA

OTTOMAN EMPIRE

Corunna

KINGDOM OF PORTUGAL

Lisbon

Douro R.

Tagus R.

Guadiana R.

Madrid

KINGDOM OF SPAIN

Guadalquivir R.

Ebro R.

Saragossa

Barcelona

Alicante

Cartagena

Seville

Cadiz

Gibraltar (to Gr. Br.)

Ceuta (To Spain)

Algiers

BALEARIC IS.

Minorca (to Gr. Br.)

Majorca

Iviza

Formentera

Corsica (to Genoa)

Sardinia (to Austria; to Savoy, 1720)

Genoa

LUCCA

GR. D. OF TUSCANY

Florence

Piombino

TUSCAN PRESIDIOS (to Naples)

PAPAL STATES

Rome

REP. OF RAGUSA

Ragusa

Corfu (to Venice)

Cephalonia (to Venice)

Chios

MOREA (to Venice; to Turkey, 1718)

Athens

Cerigo (to Venice)

KINGDOM OF NAPLES (to Austria; to Spain, 1735)

Naples

Brindisi

Salonica

Vardar R.

ALBANIA

KINGDOM OF SICILY

Palermo

Messina

Reggio (to Savoy; to Naples, 1720; to Spain, 1735)

Crete

Cyprus

FEZ AND MOROCCO

ALGERIA

TUNIS

Tunis

Gozo Malta

MEDITERRANEAN SEA

ATLANTIC OCEAN

10° Longitude E West of 5° Greenwich F 0° G 5° H 10° J Longitude 15° East of K Greenwich 20° L 25° M 30° N 35°

CHANGING OWNERSHIP OF THE CONTINENT

1682

1713

Copyright by C.S.HAMMOND & CO., N.Y.

1763

1783

ENGLISH | FRENCH | SPANISH | INDEPENDENT

FRENCH AND INDIAN WAR
1756 to 1763
Showing the division of the Country at the beginning of the war.

DISPUTED ACADIA TERRITORY

Gaspe

Prince Edward I.

Cape Breton

Tadousac

Quebec

Montreal

St. Lawrence R.

Nova Scotia

Halifax

Port Royal (Annapolis)

Canso

Ft. Frontenac

Ft. Ticonderoga

L. Ont.

L. George

Albany

Boston

New York

Philadelphia

FRENCH TERRITORY

ENGLISH TERRITORY

L. Superior

L. Michigan

L. Huron

L. Erie

Michilimackinac

Detroit

Ft. St. Joseph

Ft. St. Louis

Ft. Miami

Ft. Sandusky

Ft. Creveccœur

Fort Duquesne (Fort Pitt)

Cahokia

Kaskaskia

Vincennes

Des Moines R.

Wabash R.

Maumee R.

Ohio R.

Mississippi R.

Ft. Loudoun

Williamsburg

Tennessee R.

SPANISH TERRITORY

Mobile

Pensacola

New Orleans

Charleston

ATLANTIC OCEAN

Battle on the "Plains of Abraham" 1759

Quebec

Montreal

Isle aux Noix

Lake Champlain

Crown Point

Ft. Presentation

Ft. Ticonderoga (Ft. Carillon)

L. George

Battle of Lake George 1755

Ft. William Henry (Ft. George)

Ft. Edward

NEW HAMP.

Portsmouth

TO MASSACHUSETTS

ATLANTIC OCEAN

Ft. Toronto

L. Ontario

Oswego

Ft. Niagara

Schenectady

Albany

NEW YORK

SIX NATIONS IROQUOIS

MASS.

Boston

L. Erie

Providence

CONN.

Hartford

New Haven

Long Island

New York

Ft. Presque Isle

Ft. Machault (Ft. Venango)

Ft. LeBoeuf

Wyoming

Easton

Philadelphia

PENNSYLVANIA

Kittanning

Ft. Duquesne (Ft. Pitt)

Braddocks Defeat 1755

Ft. Necessity

Portage

Ft. Cumberland

Wills

VIRGINIA

MARYLAND

Baltimore

Annapolis

Alexandria

DEL.

THE PRINCIPAL BATTLEGROUND
IN THE FRENCH AND INDIAN WAR

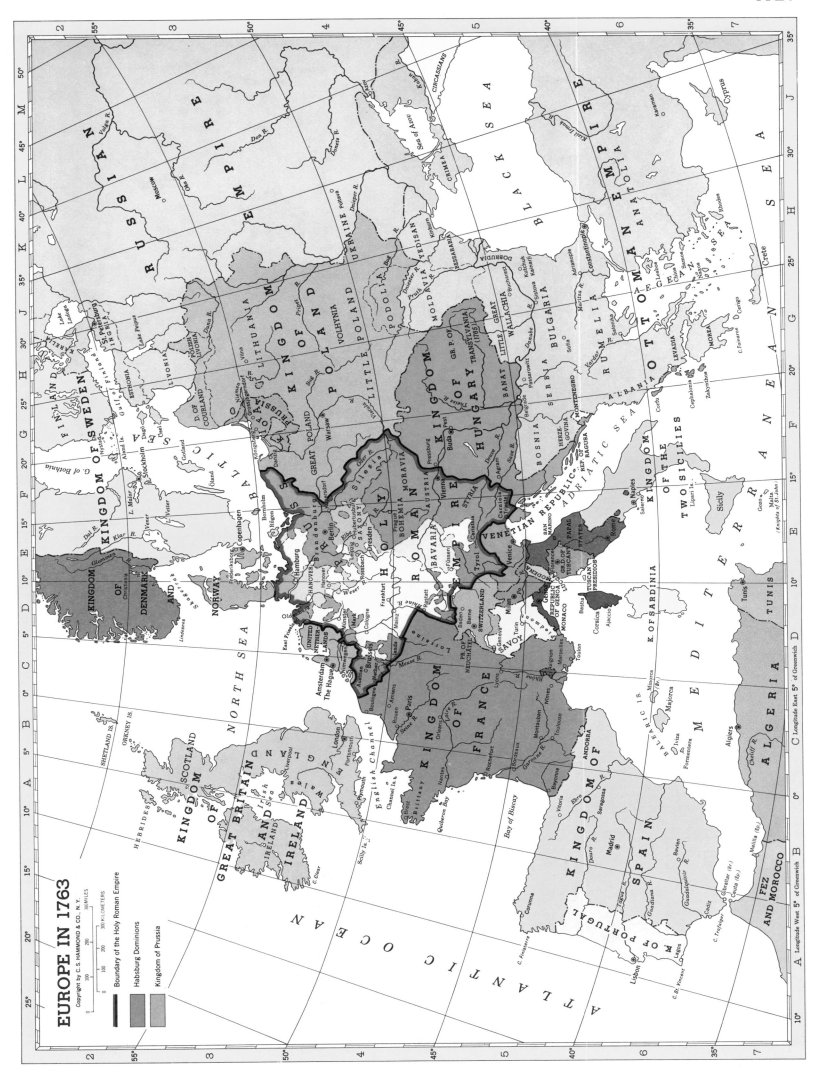

EUROPE IN 1763

Copyright by C. S. Hammond & Co., N.Y.

━━━ Boundary of the Holy Roman Empire

Habsburg Dominions

Kingdom of Prussia

MILES
0   100   200   300 MILES
0   100   200   300 KILOMETERS

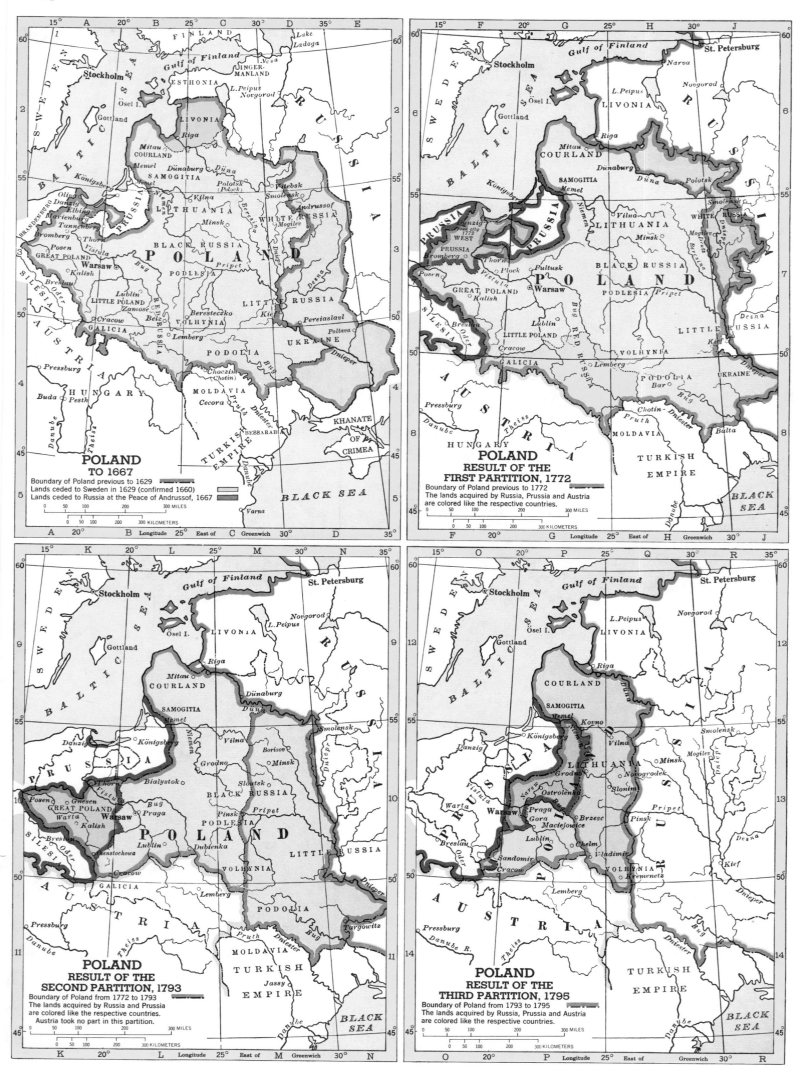

POLAND
TO 1667

Boundary of Poland previous to 1629
Lands ceded to Sweden in 1629 (confirmed 1660)
Lands ceded to Russia at the Peace of Andrussof, 1667

POLAND
RESULT OF THE
FIRST PARTITION, 1772

Boundary of Poland previous to 1772
The lands acquired by Russia, Prussia and Austria
are colored like the respective countries.

POLAND
RESULT OF THE
SECOND PARTITION, 1793

Boundary of Poland from 1772 to 1793
The lands acquired by Russia and Prussia
are colored like the respective countries.
Austria took no part in this partition.

POLAND
RESULT OF THE
THIRD PARTITION, 1795

Boundary of Poland from 1793 to 1795
The lands acquired by Russia, Prussia and Austria
are colored like the respective countries.

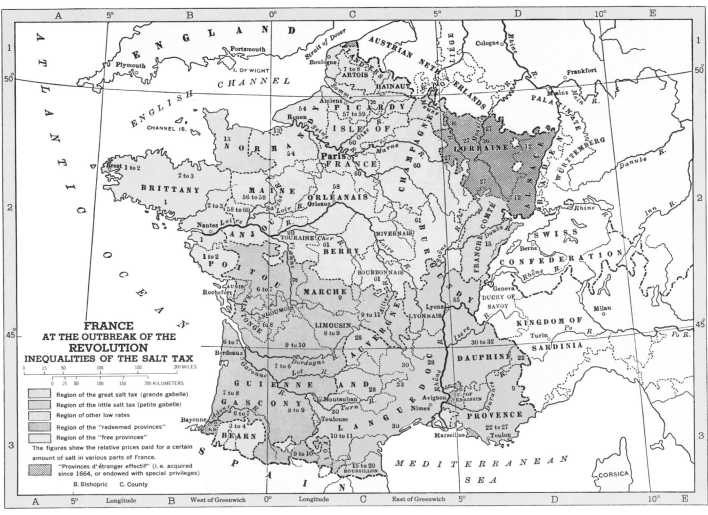

FRANCE
AT THE OUTBREAK OF THE
REVOLUTION
INEQUALITIES OF THE SALT TAX

Region of the great salt tax (grande gabelle)
Region of the little salt tax (petite gabelle)
Region of other low rates
Region of the "redeemed provinces"
Region of the "free provinces"

The figures show the relative prices paid for a certain amount of salt in various parts of France.

"Provinces d'étranger effectif" (i.e. acquired since 1664, or endowed with special privileges)

B. Bishopric   C. County

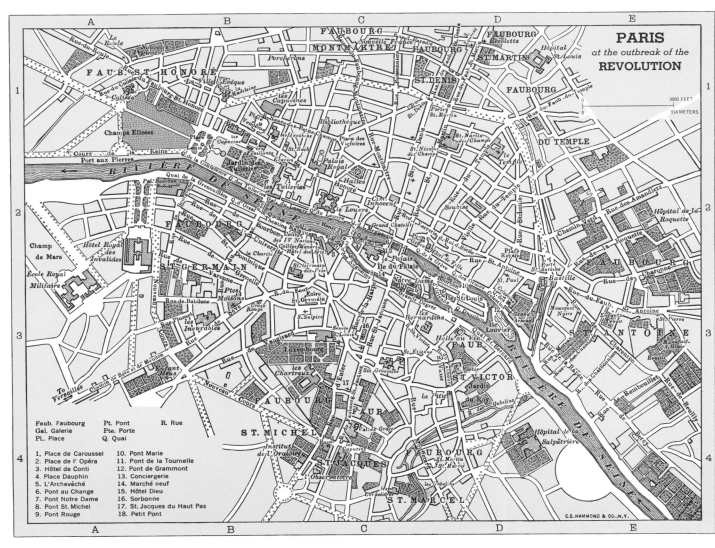

PARIS
at the outbreak of the
REVOLUTION

Faub. Faubourg   Pt. Pont   R. Rue
Gal. Galerie   Pte. Porte
Pl. Place   Q. Quai

1. Place de Caroussel
2. Place de l' Opéra
3. Hôtel de Conti
4. Place Dauphin
5. L'Archevêché
6. Pont au Change
7. Pont Notre Dame
8. Pont St. Michel
9. Pont Rouge
10. Pont Marie
11. Pont de la Tournelle
12. Pont de Grammont
13. Conciergerie
14. Marché neuf
15. Hôtel Dieu
16. Sorbonne
17. St. Jacques du Haut Pas
18. Petit Pont

C.S. HAMMOND & CO., N.Y.

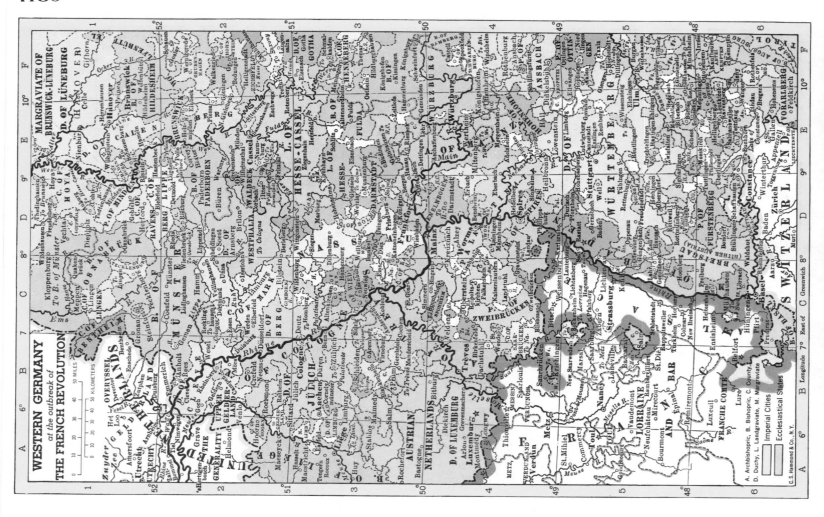

WESTERN GERMANY
at the outbreak of
THE FRENCH REVOLUTION

A. Archbishopric, B. Bishopric, C. County,
D. Duchy, L. Landgraviate, M. Margraviate
Imperial Cities
Ecclesiastical States

C.S. Hammond & Co., N.Y.

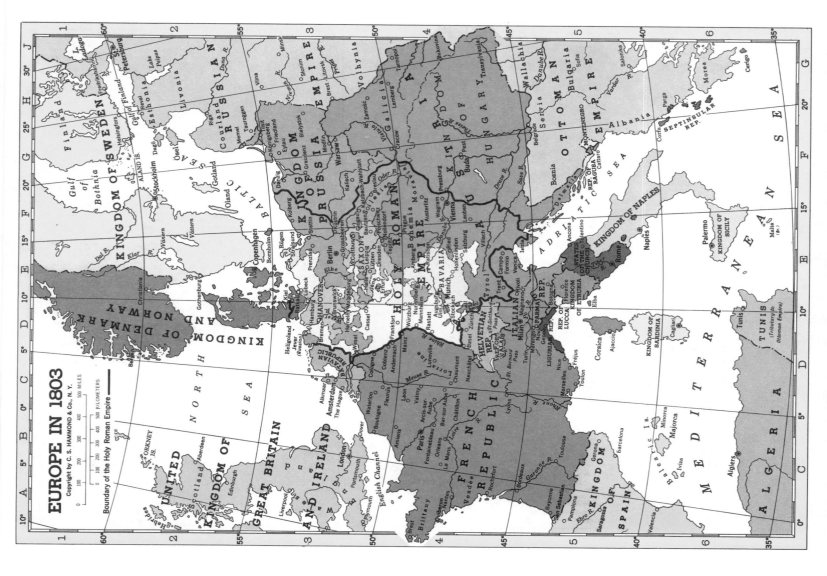

EUROPE IN 1803
Copyright by C. S. HAMMOND & Co., N.Y.

Boundary of the Holy Roman Empire

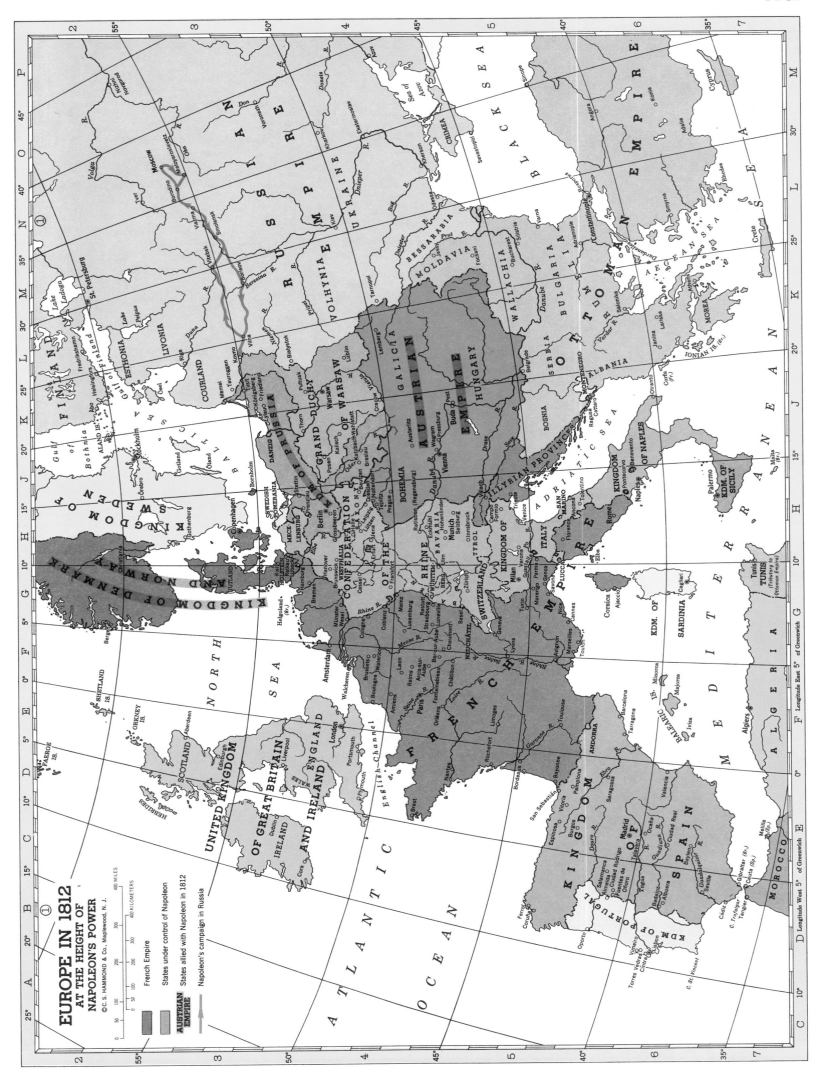

EUROPE IN 1812
AT THE HEIGHT OF
NAPOLEON'S POWER

©C.S. HAMMOND & Co., Maplewood, N.J.

French Empire

States under control of Napoleon

States allied with Napoleon in 1812

Napoleon's campaign in Russia

AUSTRIAN EMPIRE

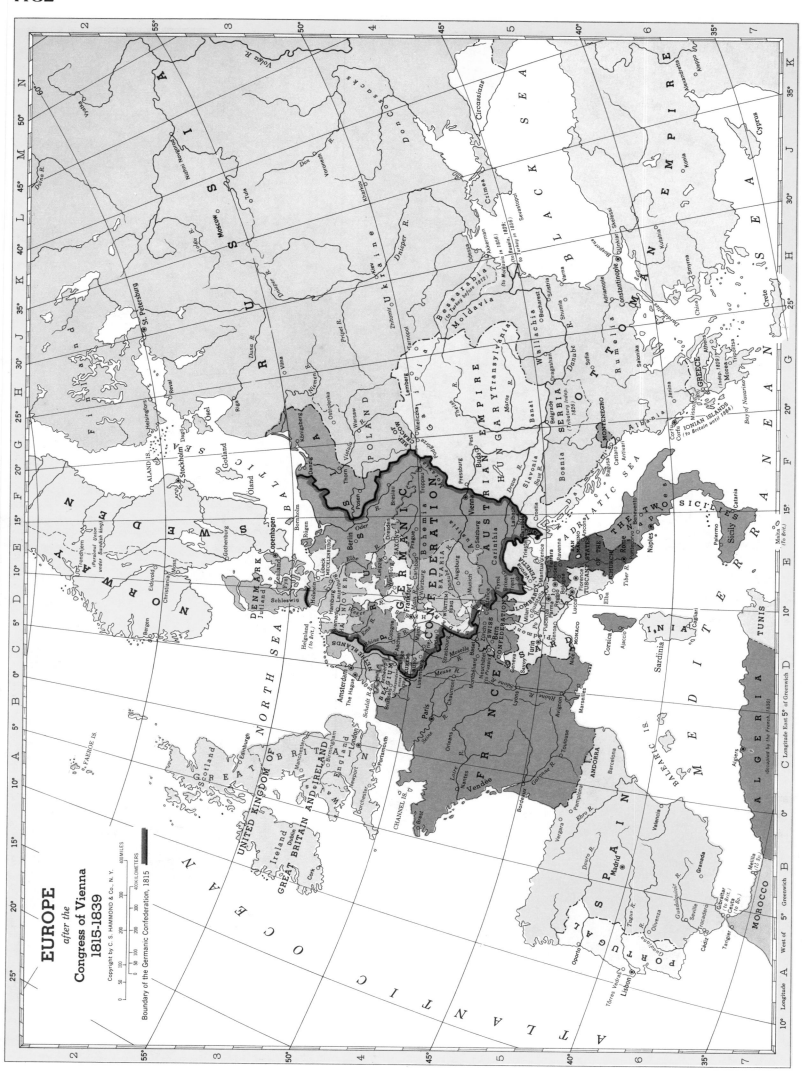

EUROPE
after the
Congress of Vienna
1815-1839

Copyright by C. S. HAMMOND & Co. N.Y.

━━━ Boundary of the Germanic Confederation, 1815

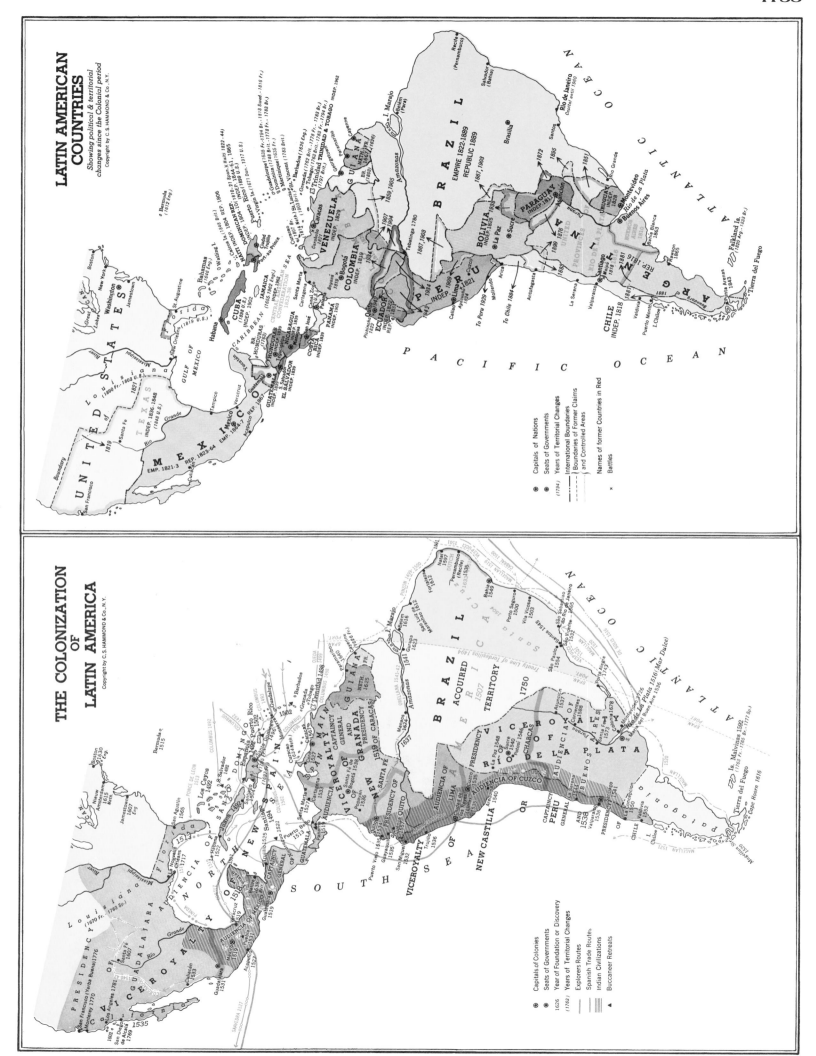

LATIN AMERICAN COUNTRIES

Showing political & territorial changes since the Colonial period

Copyright by C. S. HAMMOND & Co., N.Y.

Legend (Latin American Countries)
- ⊛ Capitals of Nations
- ⊛ Seats of Governments
- (1794) Years of Territorial Changes
- —·— International Boundaries
- —·— Boundaries of Former Claims and Controlled Areas
- *Names of former countries in Red*
- × Battles

THE COLONIZATION OF LATIN AMERICA

Copyright by C.S. HAMMOND & Co., N.Y.

Legend (The Colonization of Latin America)
- ⊛ Capitals of Colonies
- ⊛ Seats of Governments
- 1626 Year of Foundation or Discovery
- (1763) Years of Territorial Changes
- Explorers Routes
- Spanish Trade Routes
- Indian Civilizations
- ▲ Buccaneer Retreats

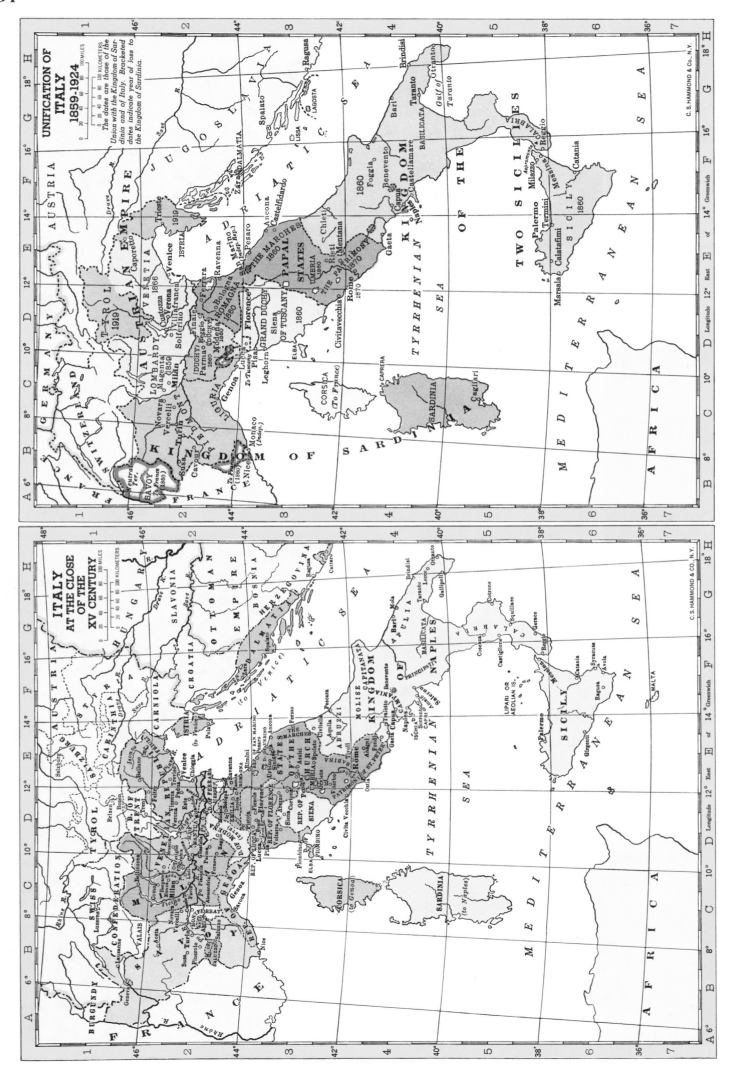

UNIFICATION OF
ITALY
1859-1924

The dates are those of the
Union with the Kingdom of Sardinia and of Italy. Bracketed
dates indicate year of loss to
the Kingdom of Sardinia.

ITALY
AT THE CLOSE OF THE
XV CENTURY

CENTRAL EUROPE
1815-1871

Boundary of German Confederation 1815-1866
Boundary of North German Confederation 1860-1871
Boundary of German Empire in 1871

0 25 50   100   150   200 MILES
0 25 50   100   150   200 KILOMETERS

Longitude 12° East of Greenwich

© The Century Co., 1932

PEOPLES OF
EUROPE
1910

Copyright by C.S. Hammond & Co., N.Y.

Longitude 10° East of Greenwich

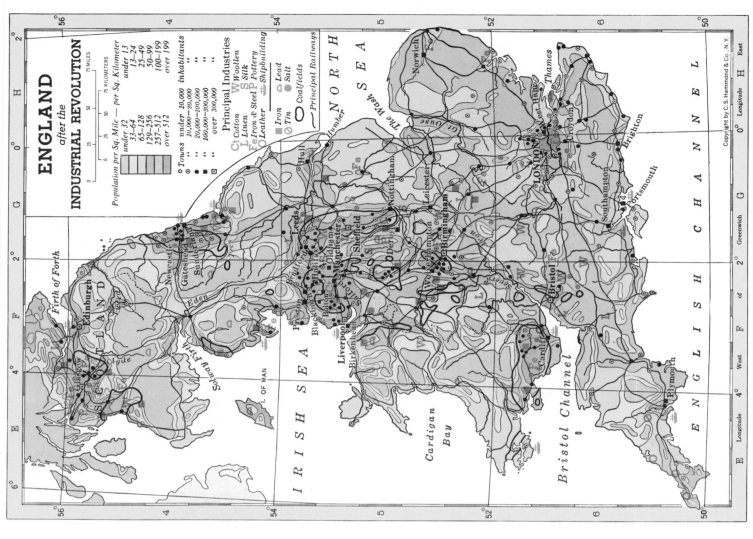

ENGLAND
after the
INDUSTRIAL REVOLUTION

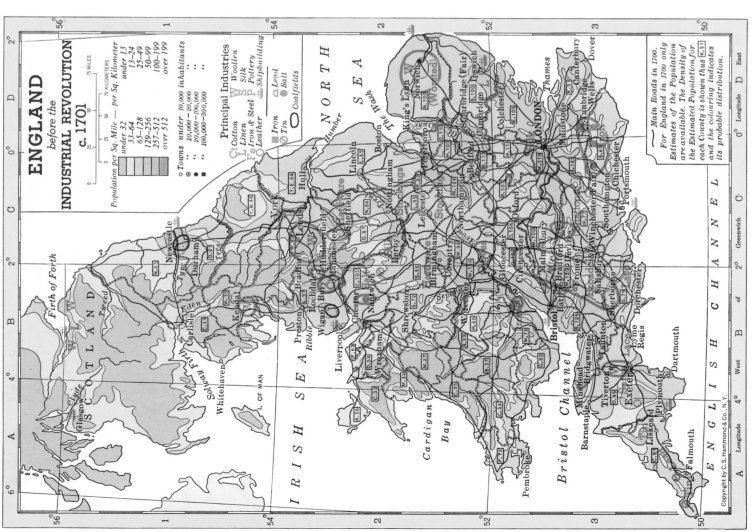

ENGLAND
before the
INDUSTRIAL REVOLUTION
c. 1701

— Main Roads in 1700.
For England in 1700 only
Estimates of the Population
are available. The Density of
the Estimated Population for
each County is shown thus K.91
and the colouring indicates
its probable distribution.

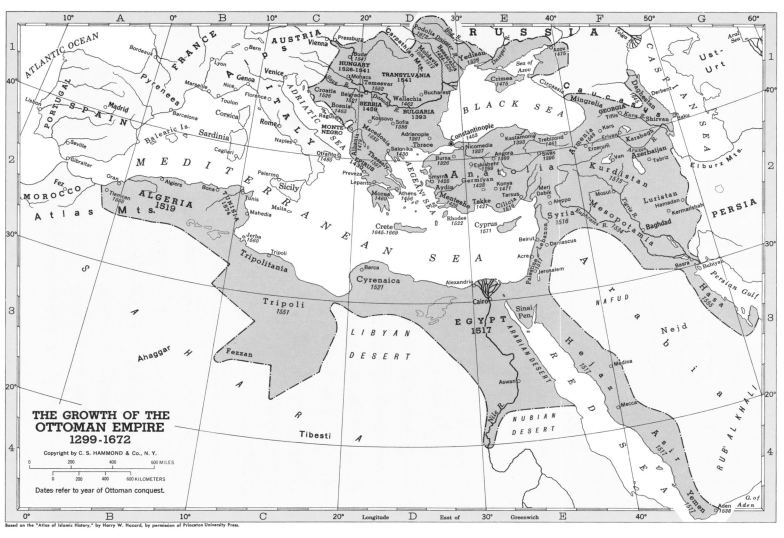

THE GROWTH OF THE OTTOMAN EMPIRE 1299-1672

Copyright by C. S. HAMMOND & Co., N.Y.

0   200   400   600 MILES
0   200   400   600 KILOMETERS

Dates refer to year of Ottoman conquest.

Based on the "Atlas of Islamic History," by Harry W. Hazard, by permission of Princeton University Press.

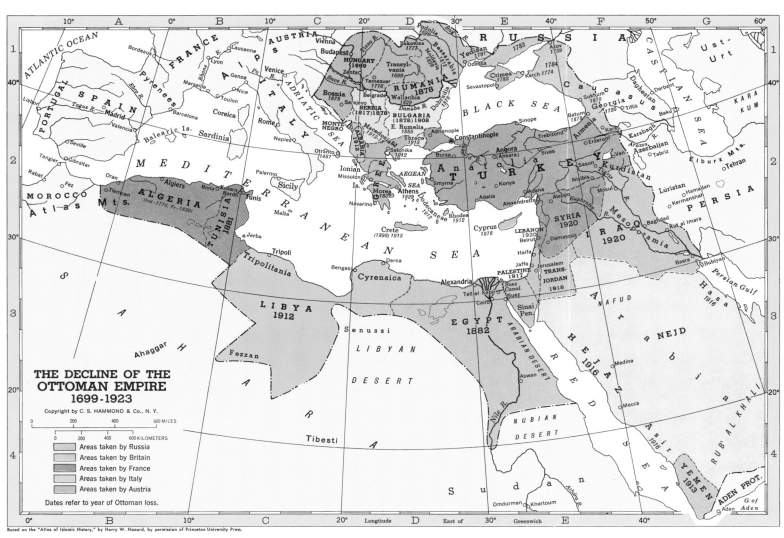

THE DECLINE OF THE OTTOMAN EMPIRE 1699-1923

Copyright by C. S. HAMMOND & Co., N.Y.

0   200   400   500 MILES
0   200   400   600 KILOMETERS

Areas taken by Russia
Areas taken by Britain
Areas taken by France
Areas taken by Italy
Areas taken by Austria

Dates refer to year of Ottoman loss.

Based on the "Atlas of Islamic History," by Harry W. Hazard, by permission of Princeton University Press.

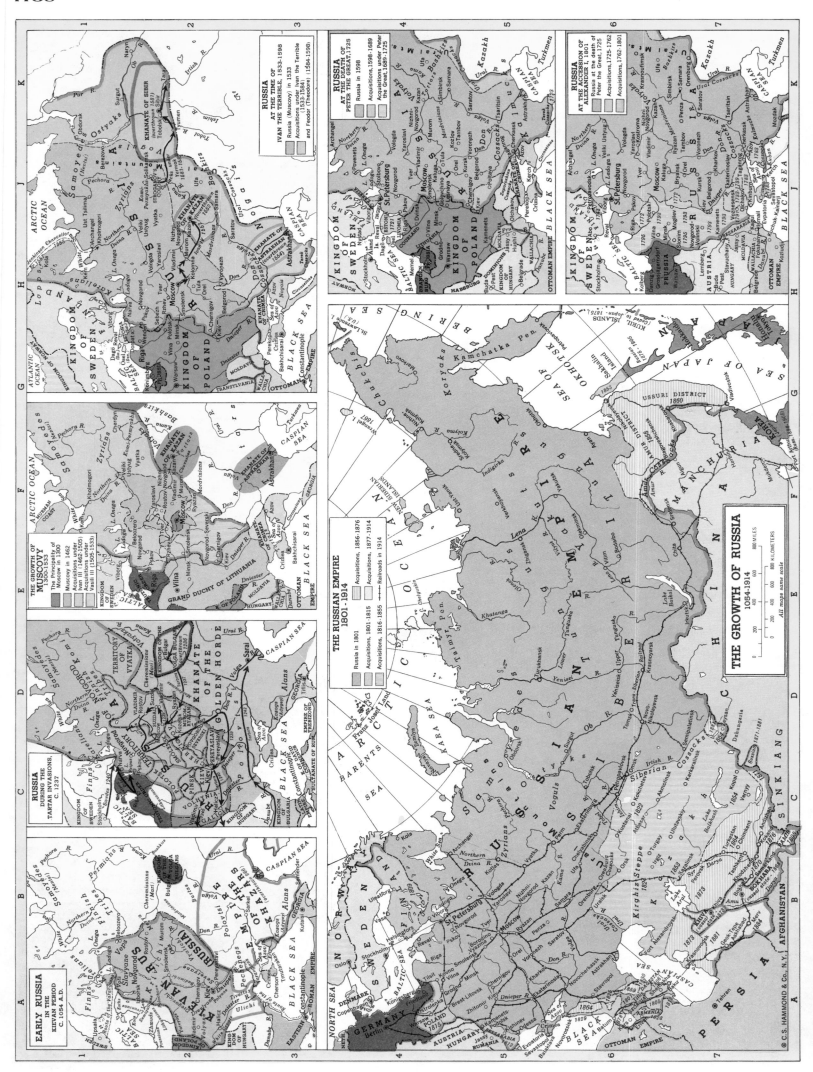

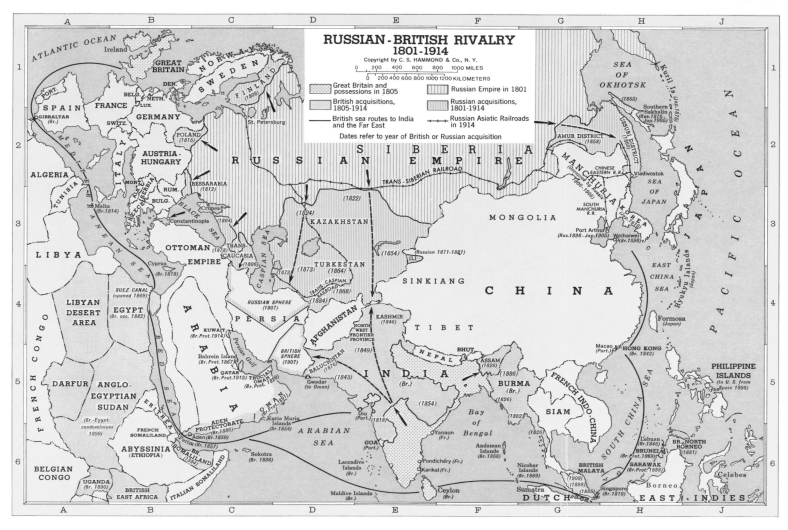

RUSSIAN-BRITISH RIVALRY
1801-1914
Copyright by C. S. HAMMOND & Co., N.Y.

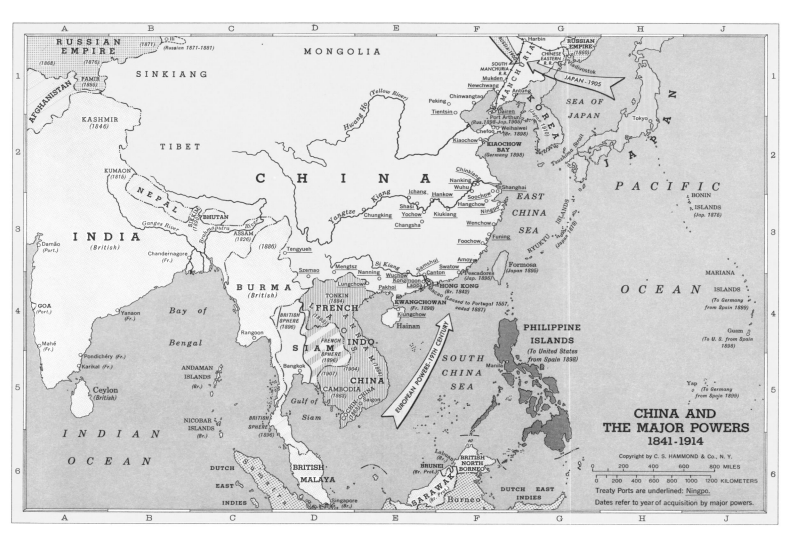

CHINA AND
THE MAJOR POWERS
1841-1914
Copyright by C. S. HAMMOND & Co., N. Y.

Treaty Ports are underlined: Ningpo.
Dates refer to year of acquisition by major powers.

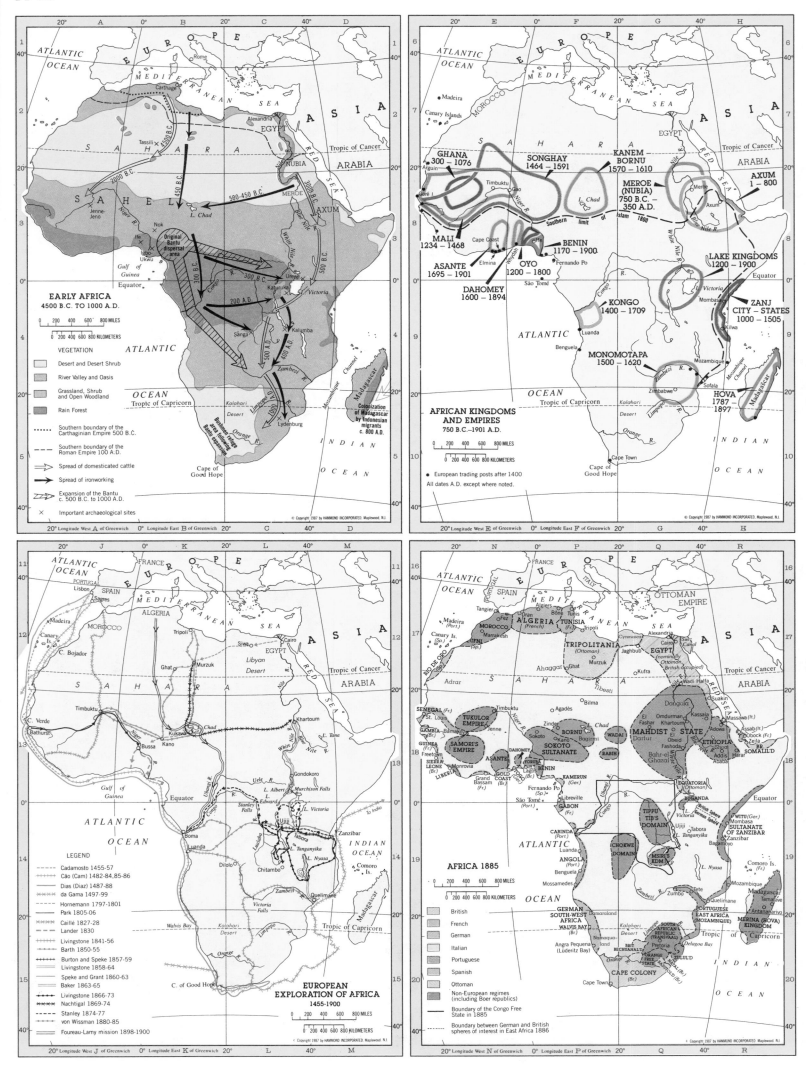

Map 1 (top left): EARLY AFRICA 4500 B.C. TO 1000 A.D.

ATLANTIC OCEAN — EUROPE — ASIA — MEDITERRANEAN SEA — Rome — Carthage — Alexandria — EGYPT — Tropic of Cancer — ARABIA — NUBIA — MEROE — AXUM — RED SEA — SAHARA — SAHEL — Tassili — Jenne-Jeno — Niger R. — L. Chad — Blue Nile — White Nile — Nok — Ife — Igbo-Ukwu — Original Bantu dispersal area — Gulf of Guinea — Equator — Congo R. — Ureve — Katuruka — L. Victoria — Sanga — Kalumba — ATLANTIC OCEAN — Zambezi R. — Tropic of Capricorn — Kalahari Desert — Limpopo R. — Orange R. — Lydenburg — Mozambique Channel — Madagascar — INDIAN OCEAN — Colonization of Madagascar by Indonesian migrants c. 800 A.D. — Cape of Good Hope

2000 B.C. — 450 B.C. — 500-450 B.C. — 3000 B.C. — 300 B.C. — 200 A.D. — 500 A.D. — 1000 A.D.

Scale: 0 200 400 600 800 MILES / 0 200 400 600 800 KILOMETERS

VEGETATION
- Desert and Desert Shrub
- River Valley and Oasis
- Grassland, Shrub and Open Woodland
- Rain Forest

····· Southern boundary of the Carthaginian Empire 500 B.C.
--- Southern boundary of the Roman Empire 100 A.D.
⇒ Spread of domesticated cattle
→ Spread of ironworking
⇒⇒ Expansion of the Bantu c. 500 B.C. to 1000 A.D.
× Important archaeological sites

© Copyright 1987 by HAMMOND INCORPORATED, Maplewood, N.J.

20° Longitude West A of Greenwich 0° Longitude East B of Greenwich 20° C 40° D

Map 2 (top right): AFRICAN KINGDOMS AND EMPIRES 750 B.C.–1901 A.D.

ATLANTIC OCEAN — EUROPE — ASIA — MEDITERRANEAN SEA — Madeira — Canary Islands — MOROCCO — EGYPT — Tropic of Cancer — ARABIA — RED SEA — SAHARA

GHANA 300 – 1076 — Arguin — Oure J. — Timbuktu — Gao — SONGHAY 1464 – 1591 — KANEM-BORNU 1570 – 1610 — Niger R. — L. Chad — Southern limit of Islam 1800 — MEROE (NUBIA) 750 B.C. – 350 A.D. — Meroe — Axum — AXUM 1 – 800 — Blue Nile — White Nile — MALI 1234 – 1468 — Cape Coast — Elmina — Ouidah — Offa — Fernando Po — BENIN 1170 – 1900 — ASANTE 1695 – 1901 — OYO 1200 – 1800 — DAHOMEY 1600 – 1894 — São Tomé — LAKE KINGDOMS 1200 – 1900 — L. Victoria — Mombasa — Equator — ZANJ CITY-STATES 1000 – 1505 — Kilwa — KONGO 1400 – 1709 — Luanda — Benguela — ATLANTIC OCEAN — MONOMOTAPA 1500 – 1620 — Zambezi R. — Mozambique — Zimbabwe — Sofala — HOVA 1787 – 1897 — Madagascar — INDIAN OCEAN — Tropic of Capricorn — Kalahari Desert — Limpopo R. — Orange R. — Cape Town — Cape of Good Hope

Scale: 0 200 400 600 800 MILES / 0 200 400 600 800 KILOMETERS

● European trading posts after 1400
All dates A.D. except where noted.

© Copyright 1987 by HAMMOND INCORPORATED, Maplewood, N.J.

20° Longitude West E of Greenwich 0° Longitude East F of Greenwich 20° G 40° H

Map 3 (bottom left): EUROPEAN EXPLORATION OF AFRICA 1455-1900

ATLANTIC OCEAN — EUROPE — FRANCE — PORTUGAL — Lisbon — SPAIN — Sagres — MEDITERRANEAN SEA — ALGERIA — MOROCCO — Tripoli — ASIA — Cairo — Siwa — EGYPT — Libyan Desert — RED SEA — Tropic of Cancer — ARABIA — SAHARA — Madeira — Canary Is. — C. Bojador — C. Verde — Bathurst — Timbuktu — Ghat — Murzuk — Ghadames — Khartoum — L. Tana — White Nile — Bussa — Kano — Kukawa — Chad — Niger R. — Gondokoro — Uele R. — Gulf of Guinea — Equator — L. Albert — L. Edward — Murchison Falls — Stanley Falls — L. Victoria — To India — Boma — Ubangi R. — Congo R. — Ujiji — Tabora — Zanzibar — INDIAN OCEAN — ATLANTIC OCEAN — Luanda — L. Tanganyika — L. Nyasa — Dilolo — Chitambo — Comoro Is. — Zambezi R. — Quelimane — Victoria Falls — Walvis Bay — Kalahari Desert — Limpopo R. — Tropic of Capricorn — Orange R. — C. of Good Hope

LEGEND
--- Cadamosto 1455-57
+++ Cão (Cam) 1482-84, 85-86
— Dias (Diaz) 1487-88
××× da Gama 1497-99
--- Hornemann 1797-1801
— Park 1805-06
××× Caillé 1827-28
--- Lander 1830
+++ Livingstone 1841-56
××× Barth 1850-55
+++ Burton and Speke 1857-59
— Livingstone 1858-64
— Speke and Grant 1860-63
--- Baker 1863-65
••• Livingstone 1866-73
××× Nachtigal 1869-74
--- Stanley 1874-77
--- von Wissman 1880-85
— Foureau-Lamy mission 1898-1900

Scale: 0 200 400 600 800 MILES / 0 200 400 600 800 KILOMETERS

© Copyright 1987 by HAMMOND INCORPORATED, Maplewood, N.J.

20° Longitude West J of Greenwich 0° Longitude East K of Greenwich 20° L 40° M

Map 4 (bottom right): AFRICA 1885

ATLANTIC OCEAN — EUROPE — FRANCE — PORTUGAL — SPAIN — ITALY — OTTOMAN EMPIRE — MEDITERRANEAN SEA — Tangier — Fez — Oran — Algiers — Bône — Tunis — Tripoli — ALGERIA (French) — TUNISIA (Fr.) — TRIPOLITANIA (Ottoman) — Cyrenaica — Alexandria — Suez Canal — EGYPT (nominally Ottoman, British occupied) — ASIA — Tropic of Cancer — ARABIA — RED SEA — MOROCCO — Marrakesh — IFNI (Sp.) — RIO DE ORO — Adrar — Ahaggar — Ghat — Murzuk — Jaghbub — Kufra — Tibesti — Wadi Halfa — SAHARA — Madeira — Canary Is. (Sp.) — SAHARA

SENEGAL (Fr.) — St. Louis — GAMBIA (Br.) — Bakel — Bámako — Timbuktu — Agadès — Bilma — Zinder — Sokoto — Kano — L. Chad — Dongola — El Fasher — Omdurman — Khartoum — Kassala — Suakin — Massawa (It.) — TUKULOR EMPIRE — GUINEA (Fr.) — Freetown — SIERRA LEONE (Br.) — SAMORI'S EMPIRE — LIBERIA — ASANTE — GOLD COAST (Br.) — DAHOMEY — YORUBA — BENIN — BORNU — SOKOTO SULTANATE — Bagirmi — WADAI — RABIH — Darfur — MAHDIST STATE — Obeid — Fashoda — Bahr-el-Ghazal — ETHIOPIA — Adowa — Addis Ababa — Harar — BR. SOMALIL'D — Zeila — Assab (Fr.) — Obock (Fr.) — Monrovia — Grand Bassam — KAMERUN (Ger.) — Fernando Po (Sp.) — São Tomé (Port.) — Libreville — GABON (Fr.) — EQUATORIA (Ottoman) — BUGANDA — British Sphere — WITU (Ger.) — Mombasa — SULTANATE OF ZANZIBAR — Zanzibar — Bagamoyo — CABINDA (Port.) — TIPPU TIB'S DOMAIN — Ujiji — Tabora — Equator — L. Victoria — L. Tanganyika — CHOKWE DOMAIN — MSIRI'S KDM. — ANGOLA (Port.) — Luanda — Benguela — Mossamedes — L. Nyasa — Comoro Is. (Fr.) — Zumbo — Tete — Mozambique — PORTUGUESE EAST AFRICA (MOZAMBIQUE) — Quelimane — MERINA (HOVA) KINGDOM — Madagascar — Antananarivo — Tamatave — GERMAN SOUTH-WEST AFRICA — Damaraland — WALVIS BAY (Br.) — Angra Pequena (Lüderitz Bay) — Namaqualand — Kalahari Desert — BRIT. BECHUANAL'D — SOUTH AFRICAN REPUBLIC (TRANSVAAL) — Pretoria — ORANGE FREE STATE — ZULUL'D (Br.) — Delagoa Bay — Limpopo R. — Tropic of Capricorn — CAPE COLONY (Br.) — Cape Town — INDIAN OCEAN

Scale: 0 200 400 600 800 MILES / 0 200 400 600 800 KILOMETERS

- British
- French
- German
- Italian
- Portuguese
- Spanish
- Ottoman
- Non-European regimes (including Boer republics)
— Boundary of the Congo Free State in 1885
--- Boundary between German and British spheres of interest in East Africa 1886

© Copyright 1987 by HAMMOND INCORPORATED, Maplewood, N.J.

20° Longitude West N of Greenwich 0° Longitude East P of Greenwich 20° Q 40° R

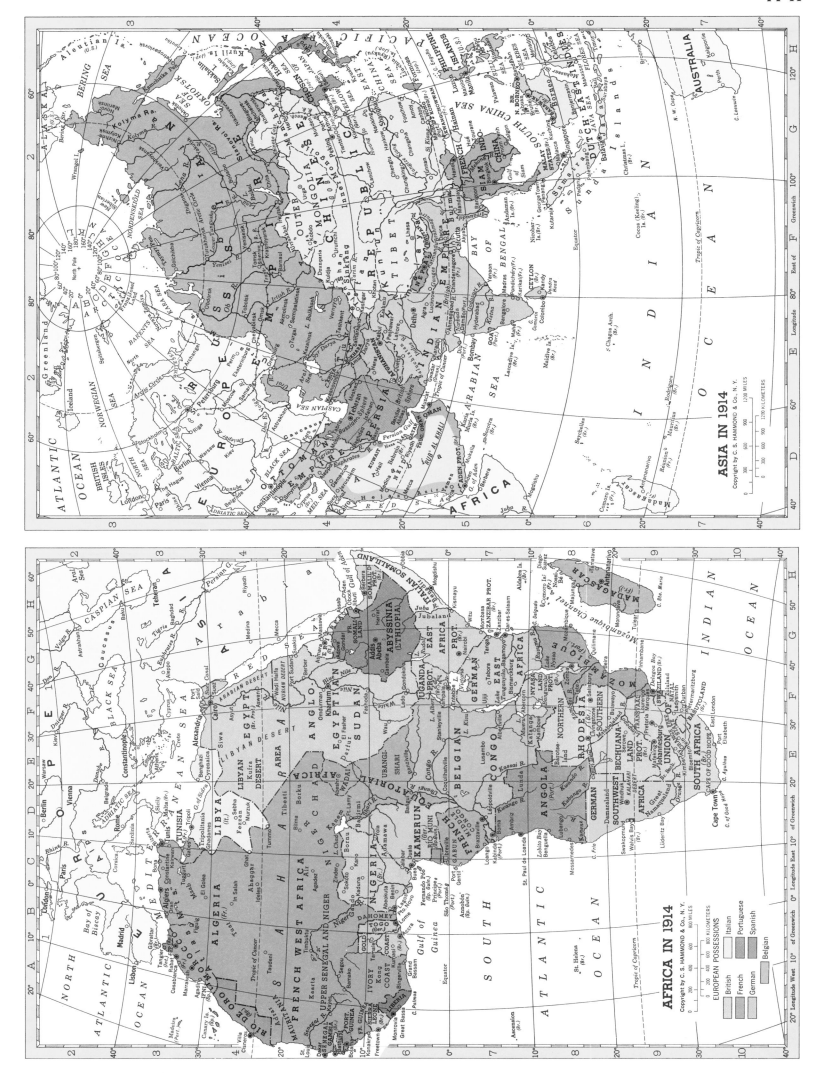

ASIA IN 1914

Copyright by C. S. HAMMOND & Co., N.Y.

AFRICA IN 1914

Copyright by C. S. HAMMOND & Co., N.Y.

EUROPEAN POSSESSIONS

British
French
German
Italian
Portuguese
Spanish
Belgian

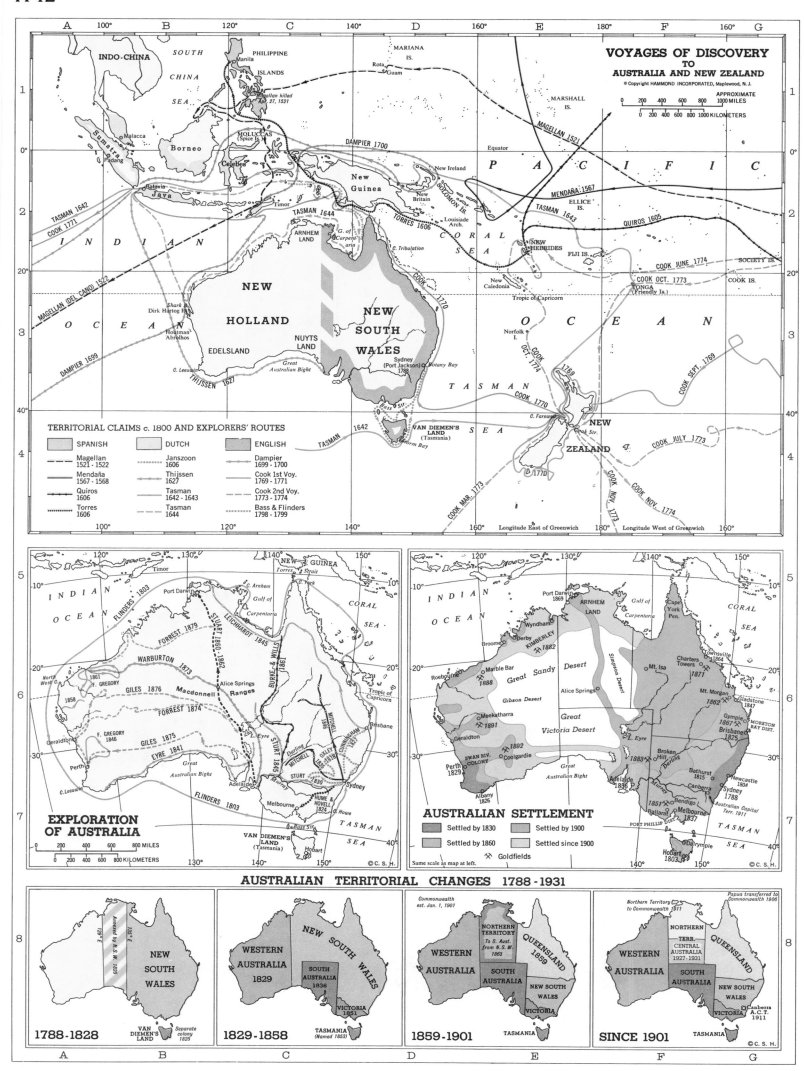

VOYAGES OF DISCOVERY
TO
AUSTRALIA AND NEW ZEALAND
© Copyright HAMMOND INCORPORATED, Maplewood, N.J.

TERRITORIAL CLAIMS c. 1800 AND EXPLORERS' ROUTES

- SPANISH
- DUTCH
- ENGLISH

Magellan 1521 - 1522	Janszoon 1606	Dampier 1699 - 1700
Mendaña 1567 - 1568	Thijssen 1627	Cook 1st Voy. 1769 - 1771
Quiros 1606	Tasman 1642 - 1643	Cook 2nd Voy. 1773 - 1774
Torres 1606	Tasman 1644	Bass & Flinders 1798 - 1799

EXPLORATION OF AUSTRALIA

AUSTRALIAN SETTLEMENT

- Settled by 1830
- Settled by 1860
- Settled by 1900
- Settled since 1900
- Goldfields

Same scale as map at left.

AUSTRALIAN TERRITORIAL CHANGES 1788 - 1931

1788 - 1828

NEW SOUTH WALES — Annexed by N.S.W. 1825 — 129° E — 135° E — VAN DIEMEN'S LAND — Separate colony 1825

1829 - 1858

WESTERN AUSTRALIA 1829 — NEW SOUTH WALES — SOUTH AUSTRALIA 1836 — VICTORIA 1851 — TASMANIA (Named 1853)

1859 - 1901

Commonwealth est. Jan. 1, 1901 — WESTERN AUSTRALIA — NORTHERN TERRITORY To S. Aust. from N.S.W. 1863 — QUEENSLAND 1859 — SOUTH AUSTRALIA — NEW SOUTH WALES — VICTORIA — TASMANIA

SINCE 1901

Papua transferred to Commonwealth 1906 — Northern Territory to Commonwealth 1911 — WESTERN AUSTRALIA — NORTHERN TERR. — CENTRAL AUSTRALIA 1927 - 1931 — QUEENSLAND — SOUTH AUSTRALIA — NEW SOUTH WALES — VICTORIA — A.C.T. 1911 — Canberra — TASMANIA

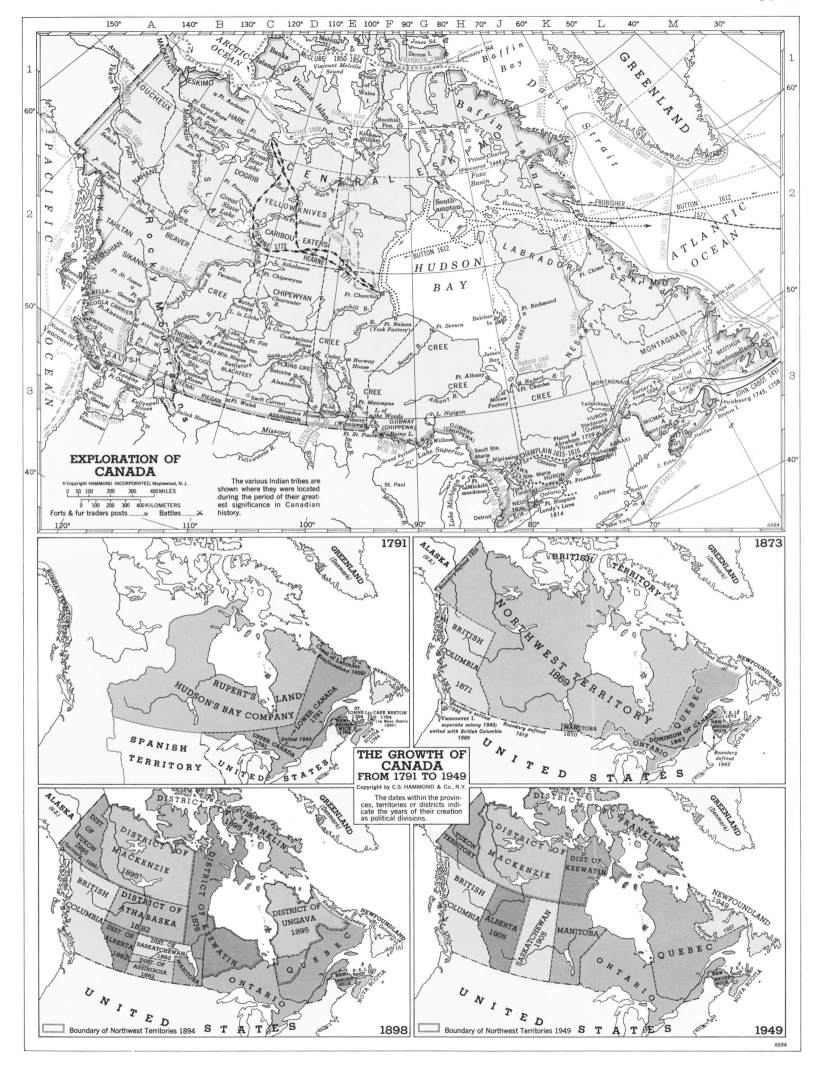

EXPLORATION OF CANADA

© Copyright HAMMOND INCORPORATED, Maplewood, N.J.

0 50 100 200 300 400 MILES

0 100 200 300 400 KILOMETERS

Forts & fur traders posts .... ⊓   Battles .... ✕

The various Indian tribes are shown where they were located during the period of their greatest significance in Canadian history.

1791

1873

THE GROWTH OF CANADA
FROM 1791 TO 1949

Copyright by C.S. HAMMOND & Co., N.Y.

The dates within the provinces, territories or districts indicate the years of their creation as political divisions.

1898

Boundary of Northwest Territories 1894

1949

Boundary of Northwest Territories 1949

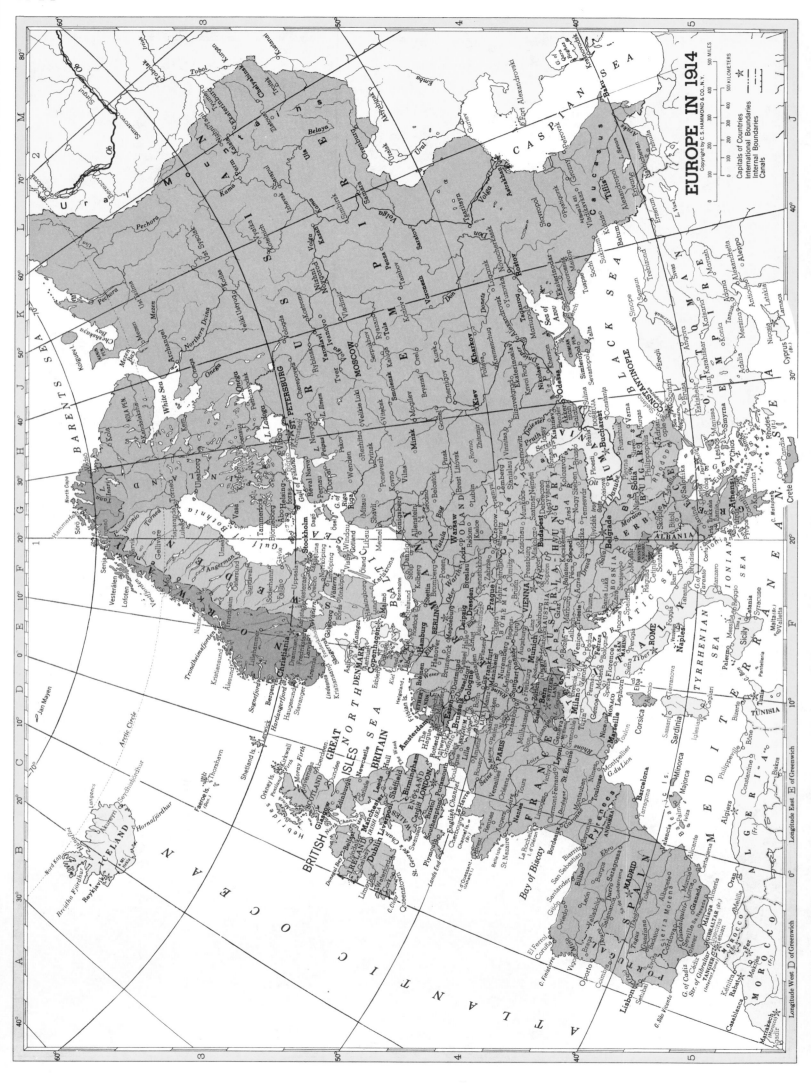

EUROPE IN 1914

Copyright by C. S. HAMMOND & CO., N.Y.

EUROPE AND THE NEAR EAST

Stabilized Line on the Western Front, 1914-1917

Eastern Front on the Eve of the Russian Revolution, Oct. 1917

Limit of Allied Advances in the East

Area Occupied by the Central Powers after Brest Litovsk Treaty, 1918

THE FIRST WORLD WAR
1914-1918

© C. S. HAMMOND & Co., Maplewood, N.J.

The Allies

The Central Powers

Neutral States

Areas Occupied by the Central Powers

Advances of the Allies

Advances of the Central Powers

THE WESTERN FRONT

Limit of German Advance, 1914

Limit of Trench Warfare, 1914-1917

Hindenburg Line, 1917

Limit of Final German Advance, 1918

Armistice Line, November 11, 1918

Limit of Allied Occupation Zone

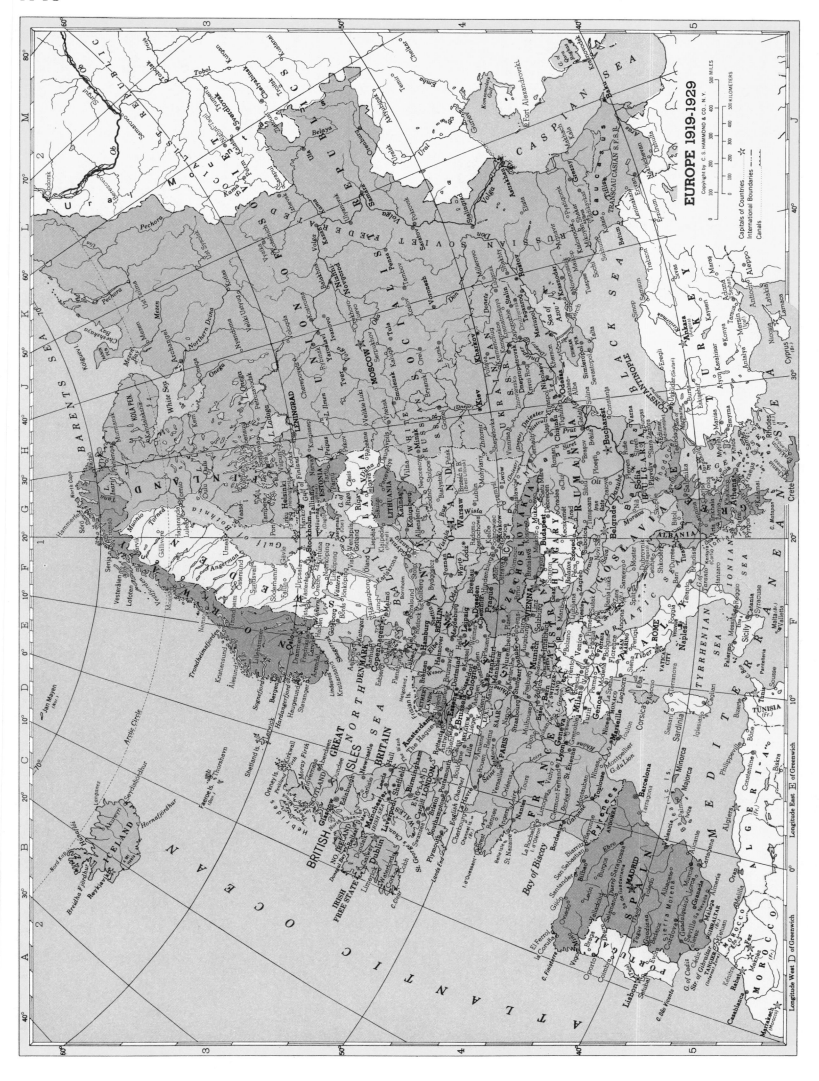

EUROPE 1919-1929

Copyright by C. S. HAMMOND & CO., N.Y.

Capitals of Countries . . . . ☆
International Boundaries . . . . . . —
Canals . . . .

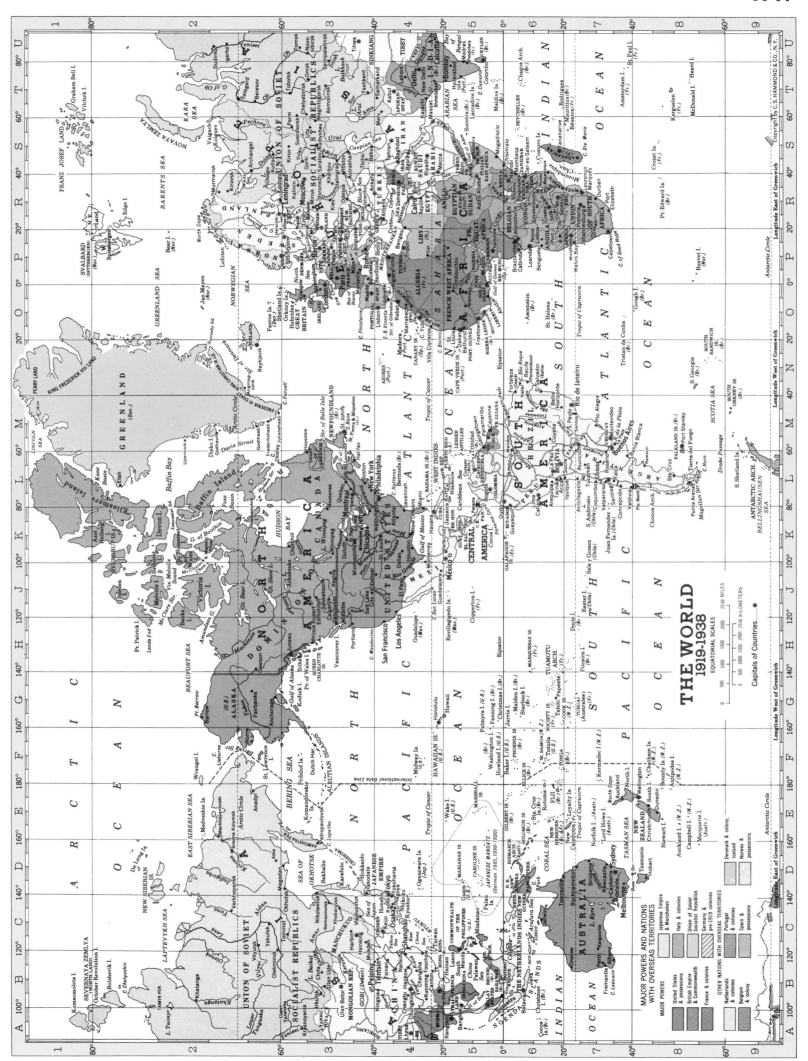

THE WORLD
1919-1938
EQUATORIAL SCALES

MILES
0   500   1000   1500   2000   2500

0   500   1000   1500   2000   2500 KILOMETERS

Capitals of Countries......●

MAJOR POWERS AND NATIONS WITH OVERSEAS TERRITORIES

MAJOR POWERS

United States & possessions

British Empire & Commonwealth

France & colonies

Japanese Empire & colonies

Italy & colonies

Union of Soviet Socialist Republics

Germany & pre-1919 colonies

OTHER NATIONS WITH OVERSEAS TERRITORIES

Netherlands & colonies

Belgium & colonies

Portugal & colonies

Spain & possessions

Denmark & colony

Iceland

Norway & possessions

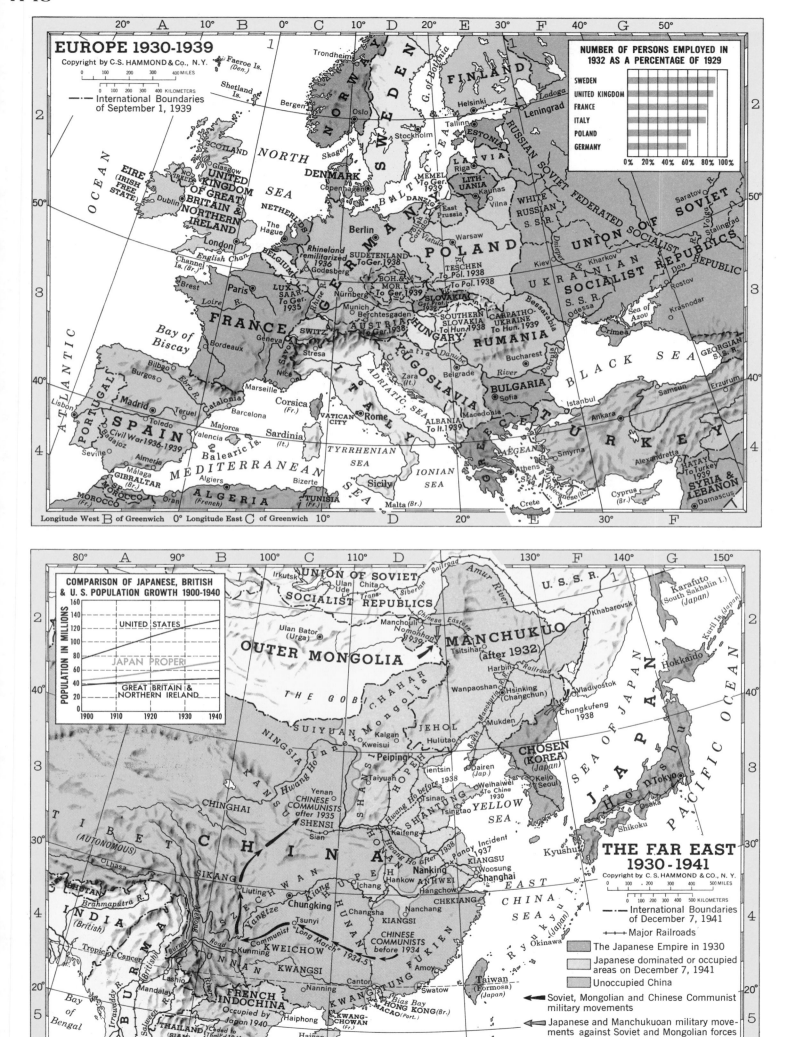

EUROPE 1930-1939

Copyright by C.S. HAMMOND & Co., N.Y.

0 100 200 300 400 MILES

0 100 200 300 400 KILOMETERS

— · — · — International Boundaries of September 1, 1939

NUMBER OF PERSONS EMPLOYED IN 1932 AS A PERCENTAGE OF 1929

SWEDEN
UNITED KINGDOM
FRANCE
ITALY
POLAND
GERMANY

0% 20% 40% 60% 80% 100%

THE FAR EAST 1930-1941

Copyright by C.S. HAMMOND & CO., N.Y.

0 100 200 300 400 500 MILES

0 100 200 300 400 500 KILOMETERS

— · — · — International Boundaries of December 7, 1941

←—→ Major Railroads

The Japanese Empire in 1930

Japanese dominated or occupied areas on December 7, 1941

Unoccupied China

←— Soviet, Mongolian and Chinese Communist military movements

⇐ Japanese and Manchukuoan military movements against Soviet and Mongolian forces

COMPARISON OF JAPANESE, BRITISH & U.S. POPULATION GROWTH 1900-1940

POPULATION IN MILLIONS

160
140
120
100
80
60
40
20

UNITED STATES

JAPAN PROPER

GREAT BRITAIN & NORTHERN IRELAND

1900 1910 1920 1930 1940

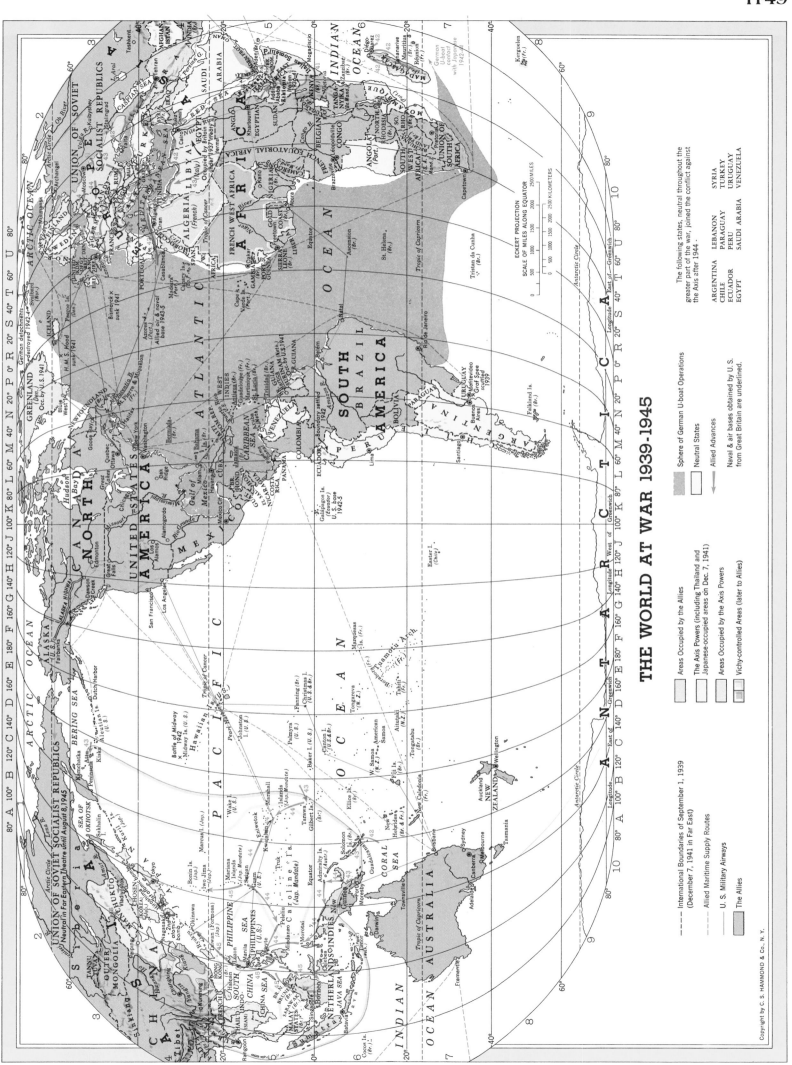

THE WORLD AT WAR 1939-1945

The following states, neutral throughout the greater part of the war, joined the conflict against the Axis after 1944 -

ARGENTINA	LEBANON	PARAGUAY	SYRIA
CHILE	PERU	TURKEY
ECUADOR	URUGUAY
EGYPT	SAUDI ARABIA	VENEZUELA

ECKERT PROJECTION
SCALE OF MILES ALONG EQUATOR

Sphere of German U-boat Operations

Neutral States

Allied Advances

Naval & air bases obtained by U.S. from Great Britain are underlined.

Areas Occupied by the Allies

The Axis Powers (including Thailand and Japanese-occupied areas on Dec. 7, 1941)

Areas Occupied by the Axis Powers

Vichy-controlled Areas (later to Allies)

------- International Boundaries of September 1, 1939 (December 7, 1941 in Far East)

——— Allied Maritime Supply Routes

- - - U. S. Military Airways

The Allies

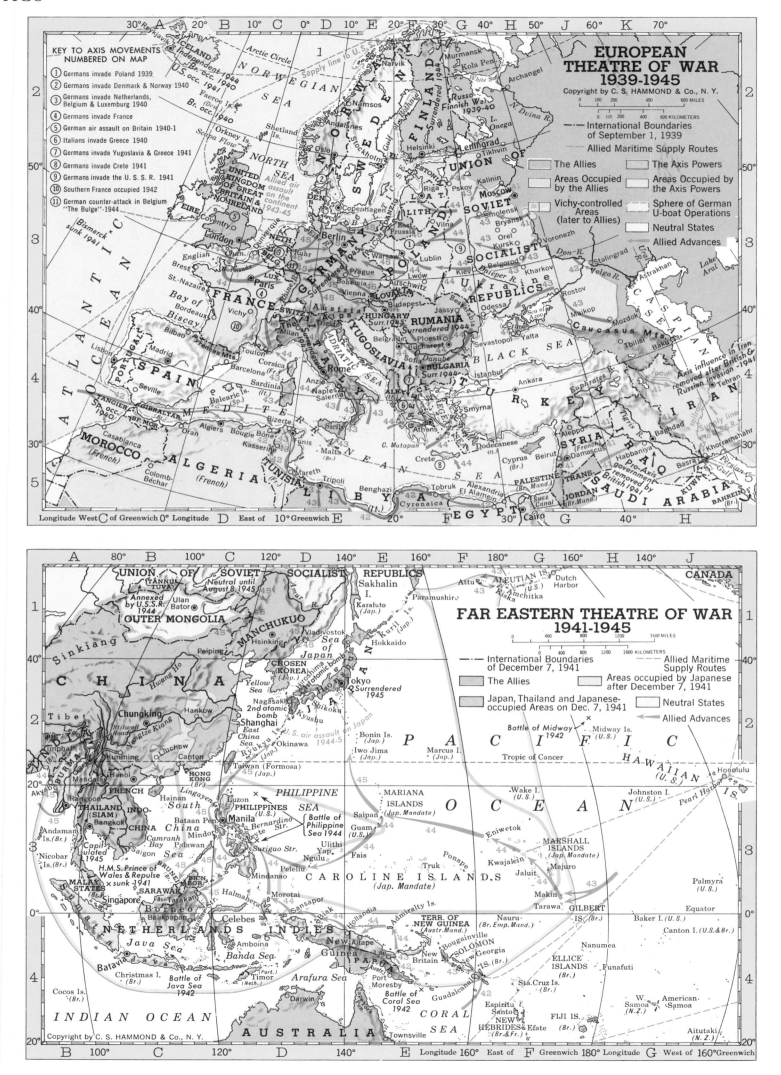

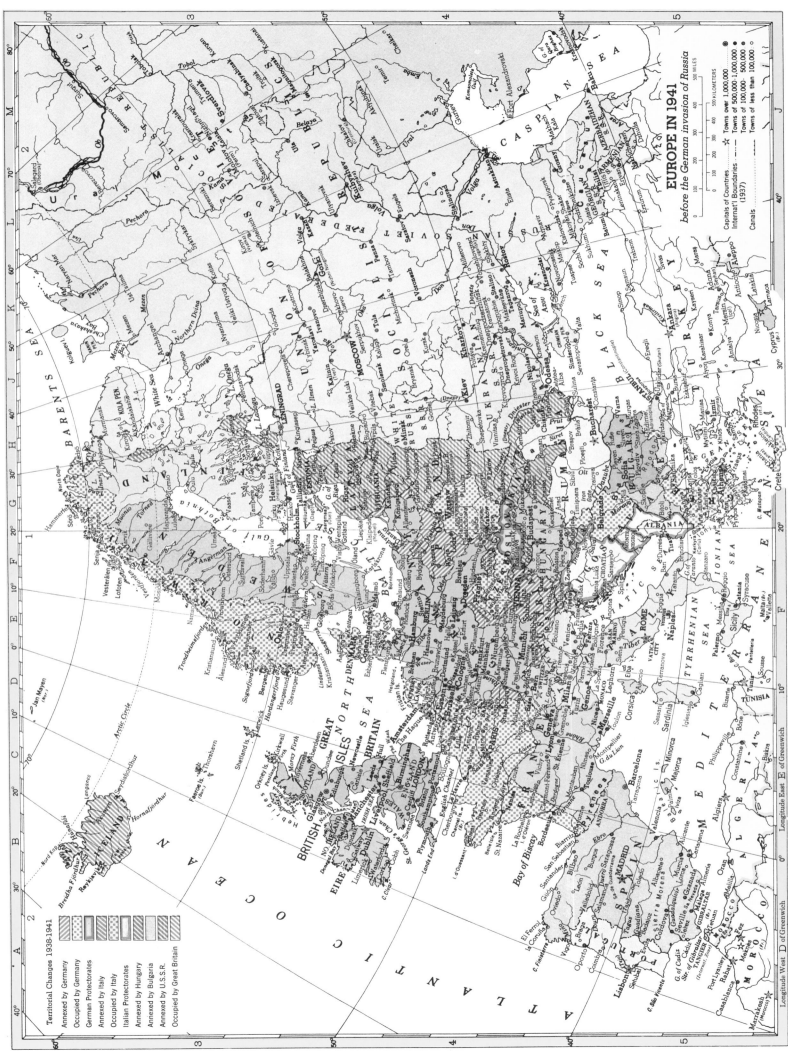

EUROPE IN 1941
before the German invasion of Russia

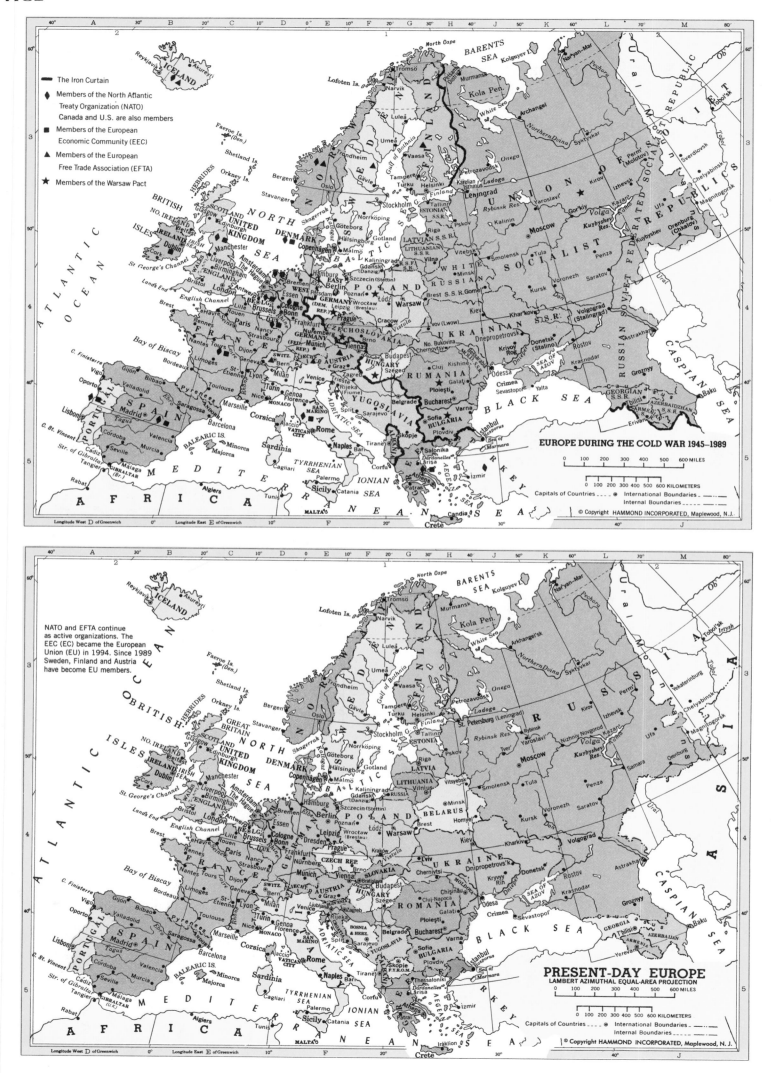

Legend:
— The Iron Curtain
◆ Members of the North Atlantic Treaty Organization (NATO) Canada and U.S. are also members
■ Members of the European Economic Community (EEC)
▲ Members of the European Free Trade Association (EFTA)
★ Members of the Warsaw Pact

EUROPE DURING THE COLD WAR 1945-1989

Capitals of Countries ● International Boundaries
Internal Boundaries
© Copyright HAMMOND INCORPORATED, Maplewood, N.J.

NATO and EFTA continue as active organizations. The EEC (EC) became the European Union (EU) in 1994. Since 1989 Sweden, Finland and Austria have become EU members.

PRESENT-DAY EUROPE
LAMBERT AZIMUTHAL EQUAL-AREA PROJECTION

Capitals of Countries ● International Boundaries
Internal Boundaries
© Copyright HAMMOND INCORPORATED, Maplewood, N.J.

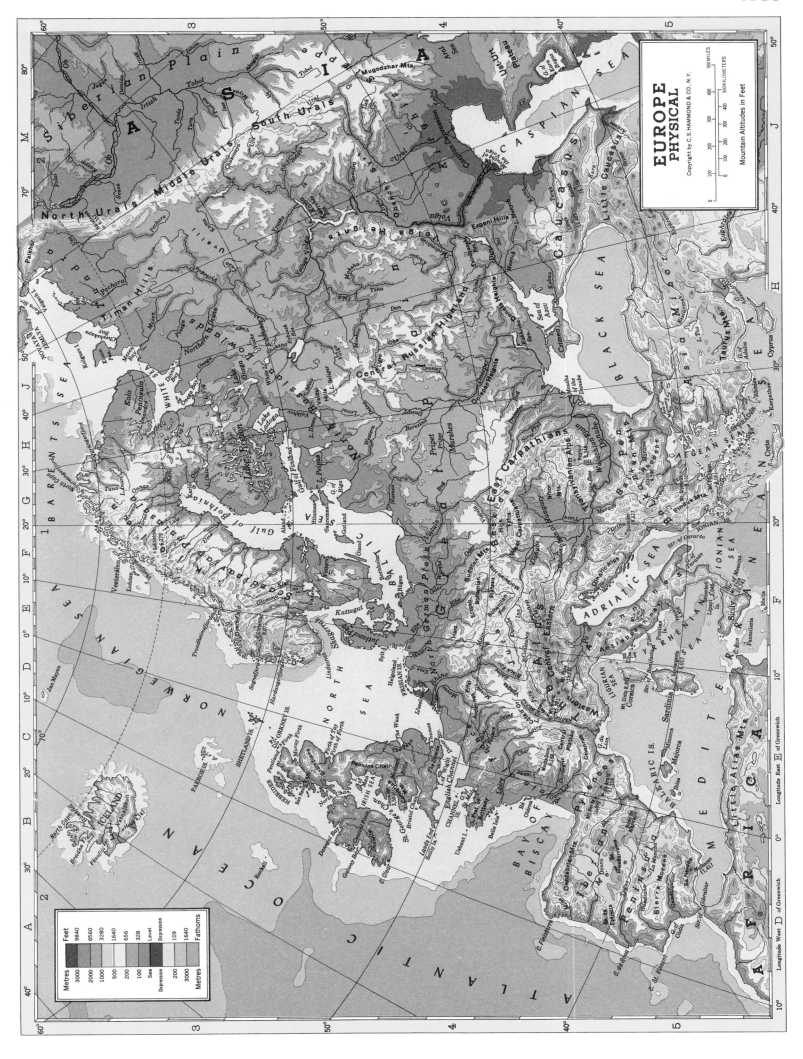

EUROPE
PHYSICAL

Copyright by C.S. HAMMOND & CO., N.Y.

Mountain Altitudes in Feet

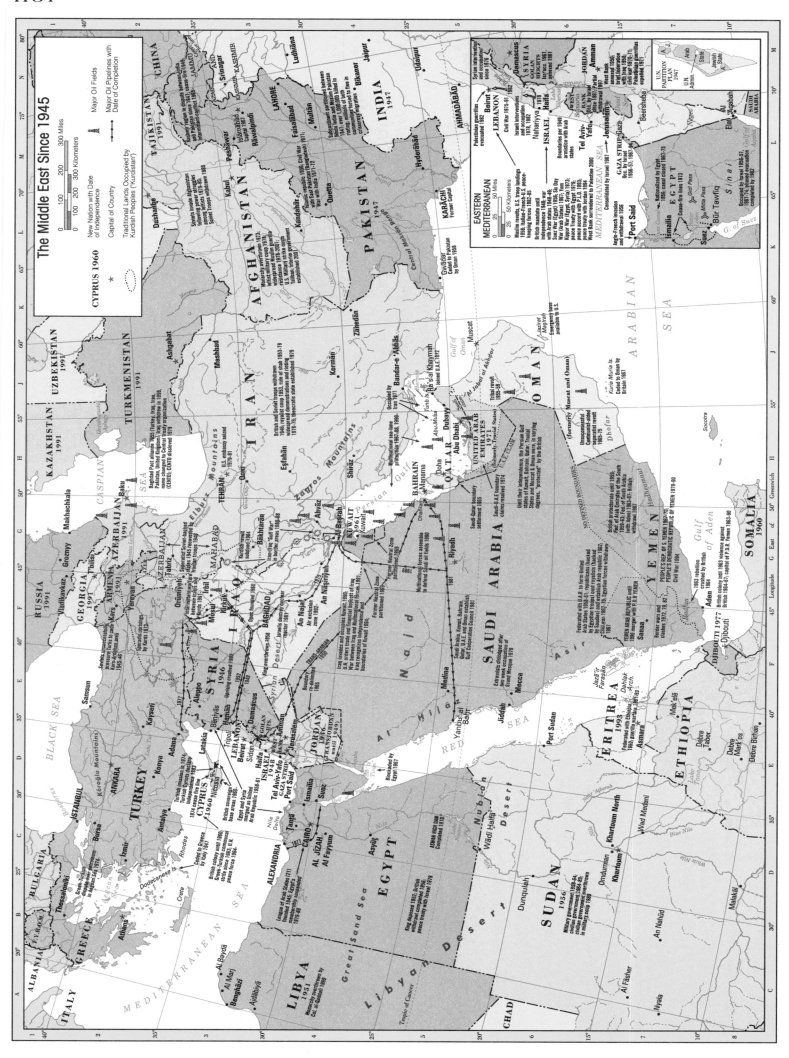

The Middle East Since 1945

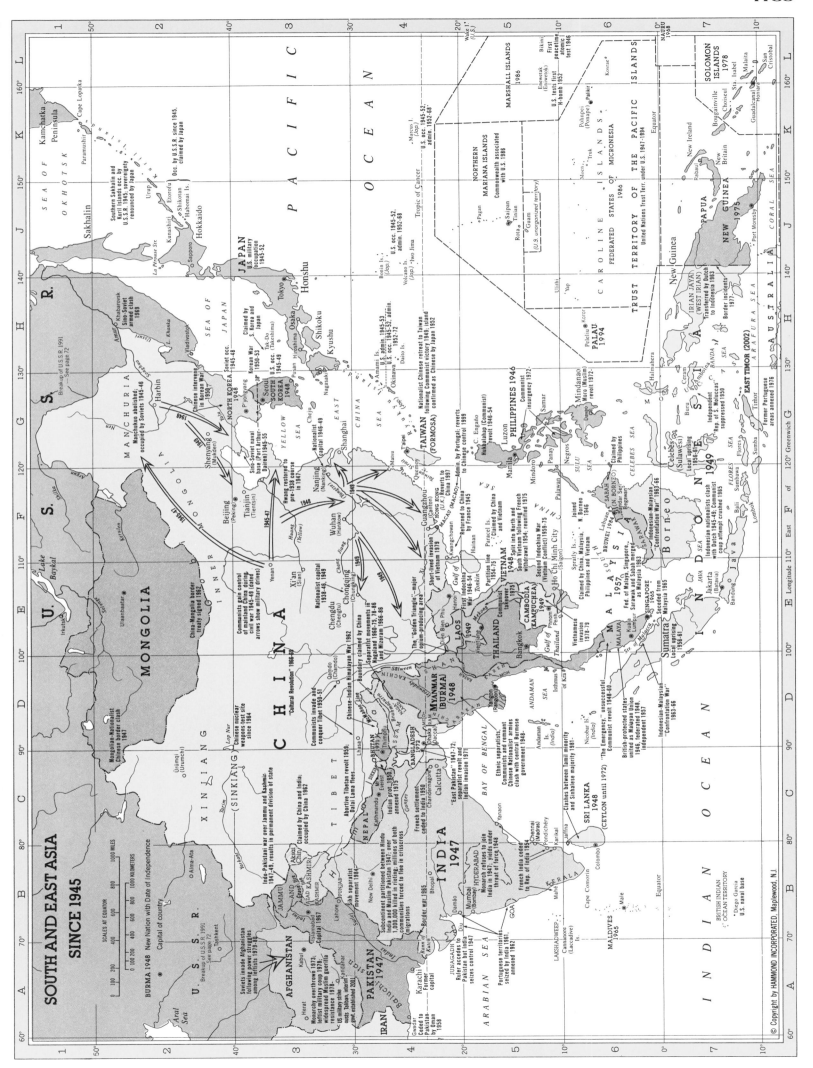

SOUTH AND EAST ASIA SINCE 1945

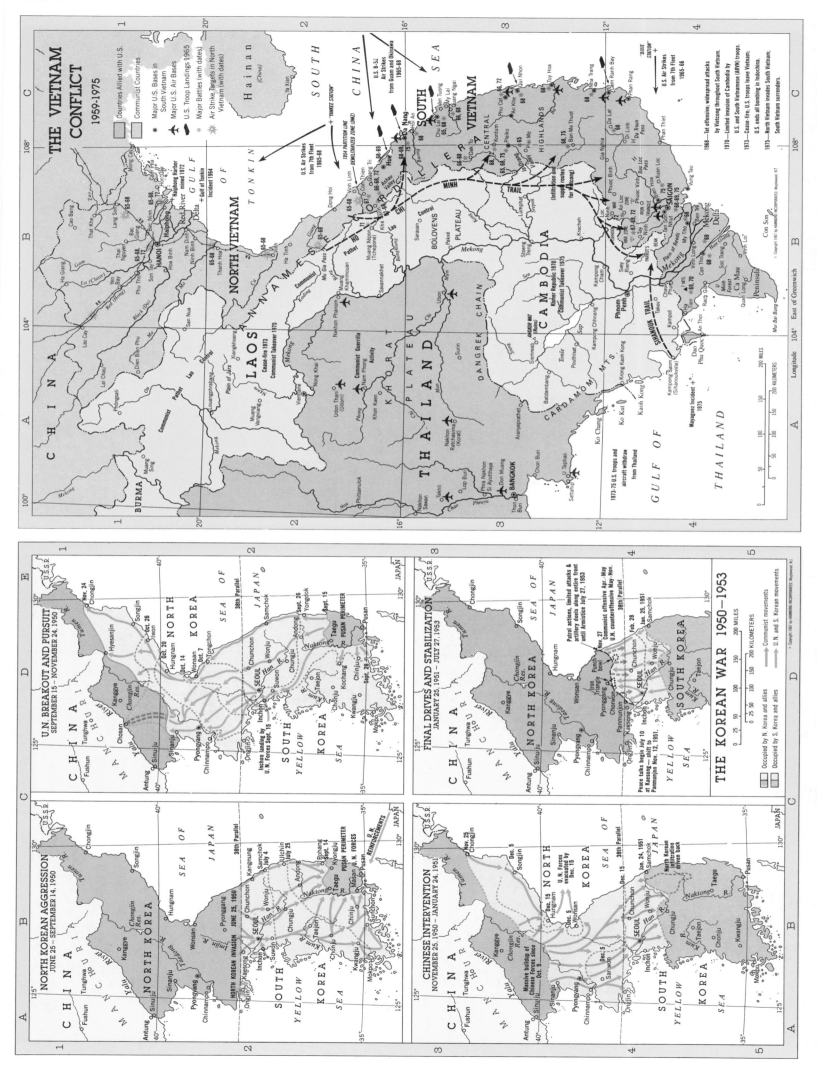

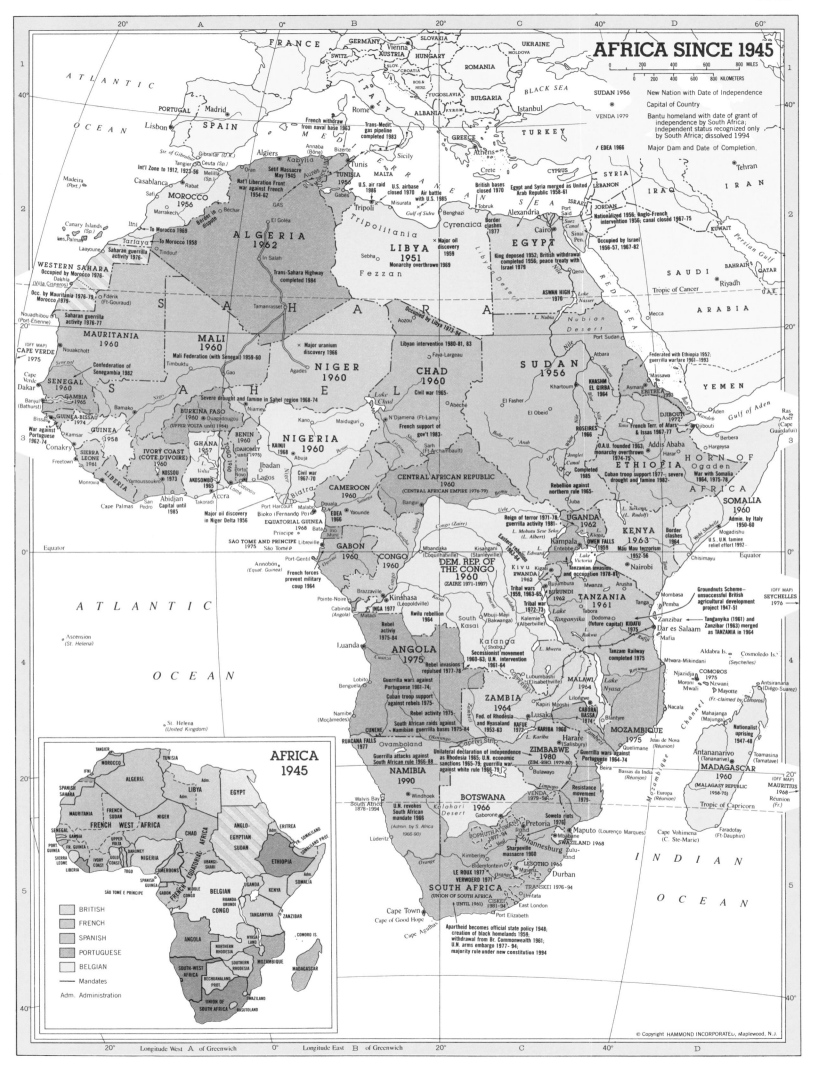

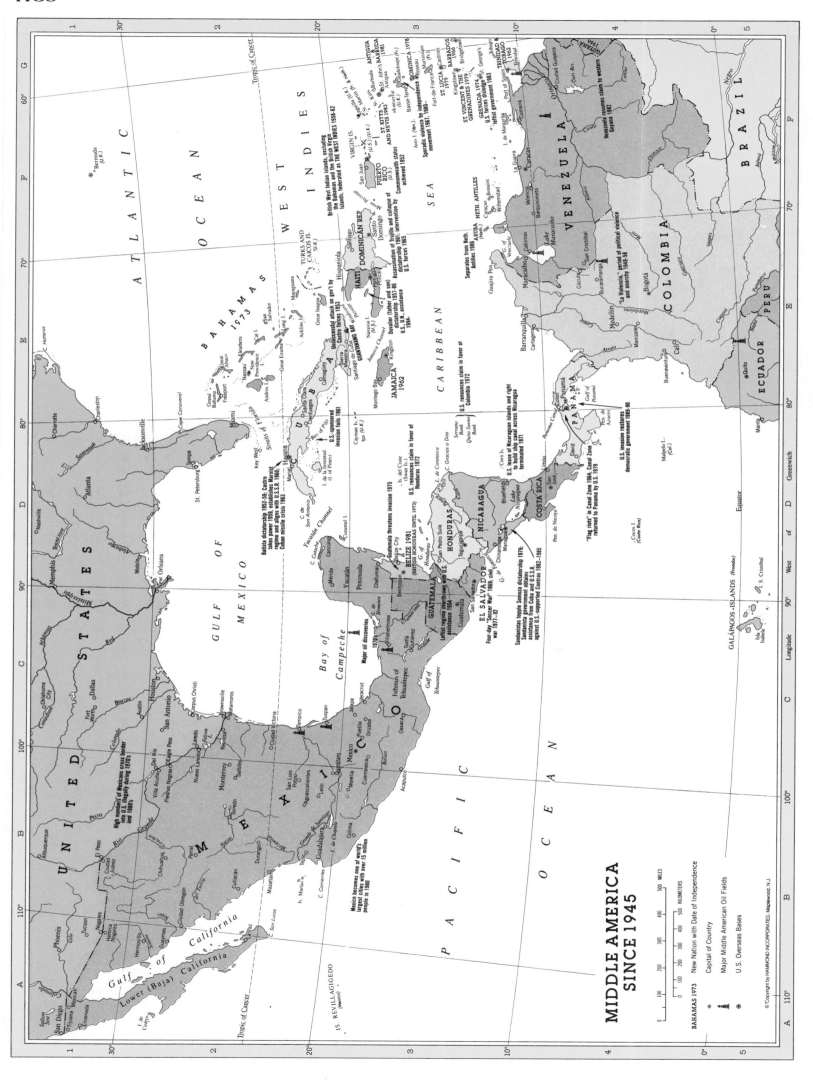

MIDDLE AMERICA SINCE 1945

BAHAMAS 1973   New Nation with Date of Independence
⊛   Capital of Country
  Major Middle American Oil Fields
⊕   U.S. Overseas Bases

© Copyright by HAMMOND INCORPORATED, Maplewood, N.J.

Batista dictatorship 1952-59; Castro takes power 1959, establishes Marxist regime and aligns with U.S.S.R. 1960; Cuban missile crisis 1962

Unsuccessful attack on gov't by Castro forces 1953

U.S.-sponsored invasion fails 1961

British West Indian islands, excluding the Bahamas and the British Virgin Islands, federated as THE WEST INDIES 1958-62

Sporadic violence by independence movement 1967, 1980—

Assassination of Trujillo and collapse of dictatorship 1961; intervention by U.S. forces 1965

Commonwealth status achieved 1952

Separates from Neth. Antilles 1986

Venezuela resumes claim to western Guyana 1982

"La Violencia," period of political violence and anarchy 1948-58

Duvalier (father and son) dictatorship 1957-86; U.S., U.N. assistance 1994—

U.S. renounces claim in favor of Colombia 1912

U.S. renounces claim in favor of Honduras 1972

U.S. lease of Nicaraguan islands and right to build ship canal across Nicaragua terminated 1971

"Flag riots" in Canal Zone 1964; Canal Zone returned to Panama by U.S. 1979

U.S. invasion restores democratic government 1989-90

Sandinistas topple Somoza dictatorship 1979; Sandinista government obtains assistance from Cuba and U.S.S.R. against U.S.-supported Contras 1982-1985

Four-day "Soccer War" 1969; civil war 1977-92

Leftist regime overthrown with U.S. assistance 1954

Guatemala threatens invasion 1975

BELIZE 1981 (BRITISH HONDURAS UNTIL 1973)

Major oil discoveries 1970's

High numbers of Mexicans cross border into U.S. illegally during 1970's and 1980's

Mexico becomes one of world's largest cities with over 15 million people in 1980

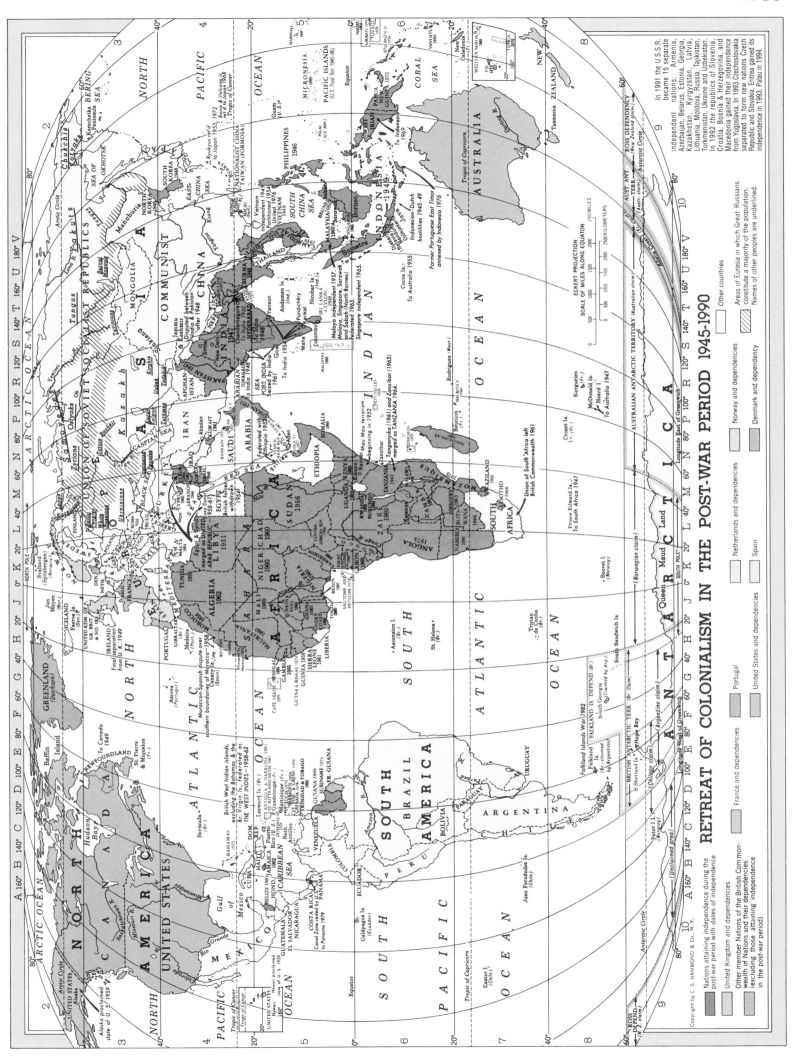

RETREAT OF COLONIALISM IN THE POST-WAR PERIOD 1945-1990

In 1991 the U.S.S.R. became 15 separate nations:

Independent nations: Armenia, Azerbaijan, Belarus, Estonia, Georgia, Kazakhstan, Kyrgyzstan, Latvia, Lithuania, Moldova, Russia, Tajikistan, Turkmenistan, Ukraine and Uzbekistan. In 1992 the republics of Slovenia, Croatia, Bosnia & Herzegovina, and Macedonia gained their independence from Yugoslavia. In 1993 Czechoslovakia separated to form new nations Czech Republic and Slovakia. Eritrea gained its independence in 1993. Palau in 1994.

ECKERT PROJECTION
SCALE OF MILES ALONG EQUATOR

Areas of Eurasia in which Great Russians constitute a majority of the population.
Names of other peoples are underlined.

Other countries

Norway and dependencies

Denmark and dependency

Portugal

United States and dependencies

Spain

France and dependencies

United Kingdom and dependencies

Other member Nations of the British Commonwealth of Nations and their dependencies (excluding those attaining independence in the post-war period)

Nations attaining independence during the post-war period with dates of independence

Netherlands and dependencies

Copyright by C. S. HAMMOND & Co., N.Y.

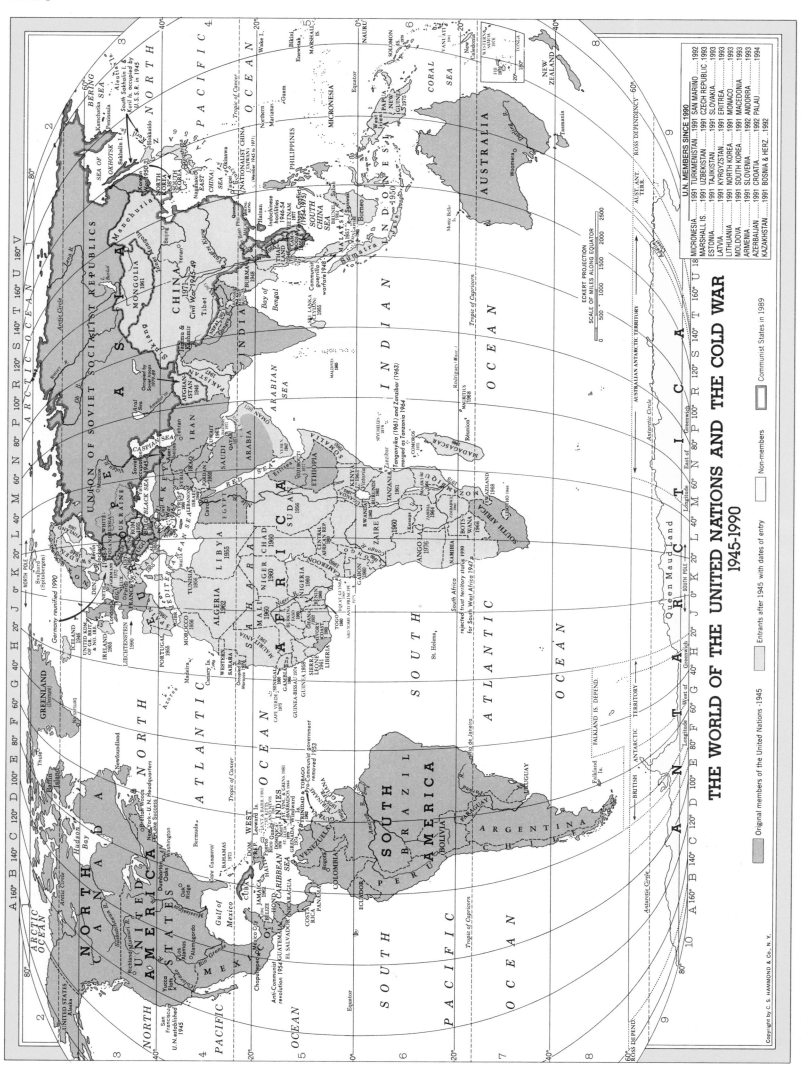

THE WORLD OF THE UNITED NATIONS AND THE COLD WAR
1945-1990

U.N. MEMBERS SINCE 1990			
MICRONESIA	1991	TURKMENISTAN	1992
MARSHALL IS.	1991	UZBEKISTAN	1992
ESTONIA	1991	SAN MARINO	1992
LATVIA	1991	CZECH REPUBLIC	1993
LITHUANIA	1991	SLOVAKIA	1993
MOLDOVA	1991	ERITREA	1993
ARMENIA	1991	MONACO	1993
AZERBAIJAN	1991	NORTH KOREA	1993
KAZAKHSTAN	1991	SOUTH KOREA	1993
TAJIKISTAN	1991	MACEDONIA	1993
KYRGYZSTAN	1991	ANDORRA	1993
		SLOVENIA	1992
		CROATIA	1992
		PALAU	1994
		BOSNIA & HERZ.	1992

Original members of the United Nations -1945

Entrants after 1945 with dates of entry

Non-members

Communist States in 1989

SCALE OF MILES ALONG EQUATOR
ECKERT PROJECTION

Copyright by C. S. HAMMOND & CO., N.Y.

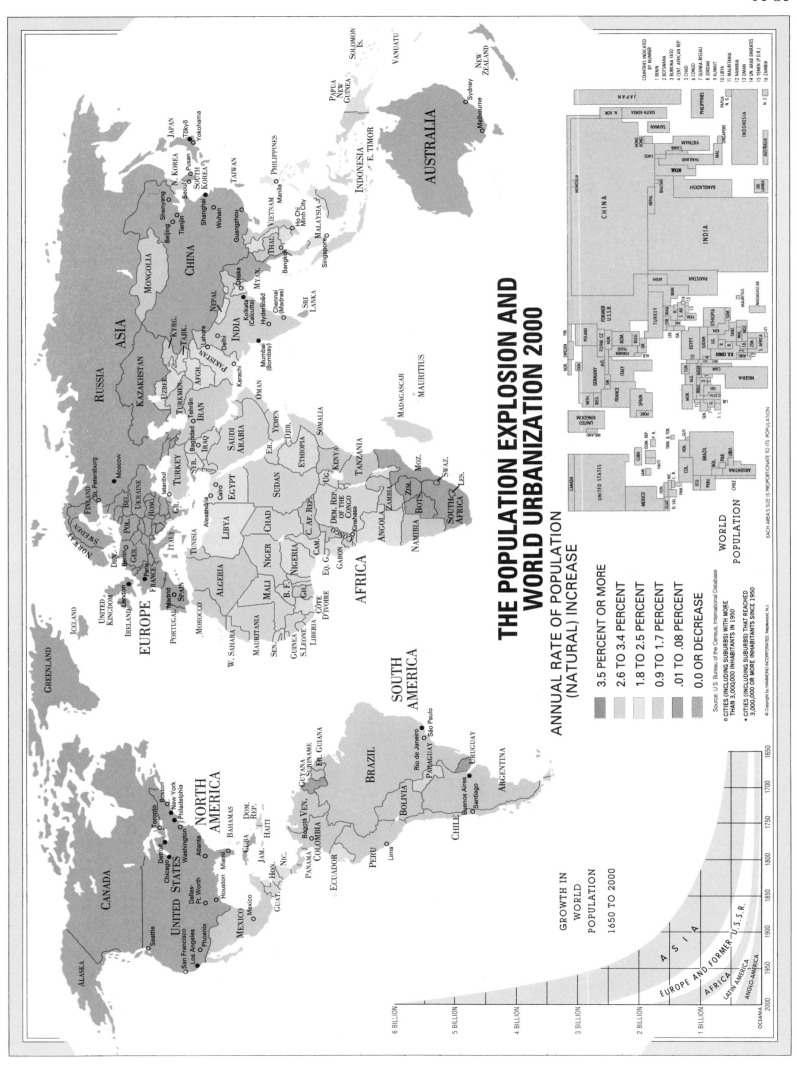

THE POPULATION EXPLOSION AND WORLD URBANIZATION 2000

ANNUAL RATE OF POPULATION (NATURAL) INCREASE

- 3.5 PERCENT OR MORE
- 2.6 TO 3.4 PERCENT
- 1.8 TO 2.5 PERCENT
- 0.9 TO 1.7 PERCENT
- .01 TO .08 PERCENT
- 0.0 OR DECREASE

Source: U.S. Bureau of the Census, International Database

○ CITIES (INCLUDING SUBURBS) WITH MORE THAN 3,000,000 INHABITANTS IN 1950

● CITIES (INCLUDING SUBURBS) THAT REACHED 3,000,000 OR MORE INHABITANTS SINCE 1950

© Copyright by HAMMOND INCORPORATED, Maplewood, N.J.

WORLD POPULATION

EACH AREA'S SIZE IS PROPORTIONATE TO ITS POPULATION

COUNTRIES INDICATED BY NUMBER
1 BENIN
2 BOTSWANA
3 BURKINA FASO
4 CENT. AFRICAN REP
5 CHAD
6 CONGO
7 GUINEA-BISSAU
8 JORDAN
9 KUWAIT
10 LIBYA
11 MAURITANIA
12 NAMIBIA
13 OMAN
14 UN ARAB EMIRATES
15 YEMEN (P.D.R.)
16 ZAMBIA

GROWTH IN WORLD POPULATION 1650 TO 2000

	1650	1700	1750	1800	1850	1900	1950	2000
6 BILLION								
5 BILLION								
4 BILLION								
3 BILLION								
2 BILLION								
1 BILLION								

ASIA
EUROPE AND FORMER U.S.S.R.
AFRICA
LATIN AMERICA
ANGLO-AMERICA
OCEANIA

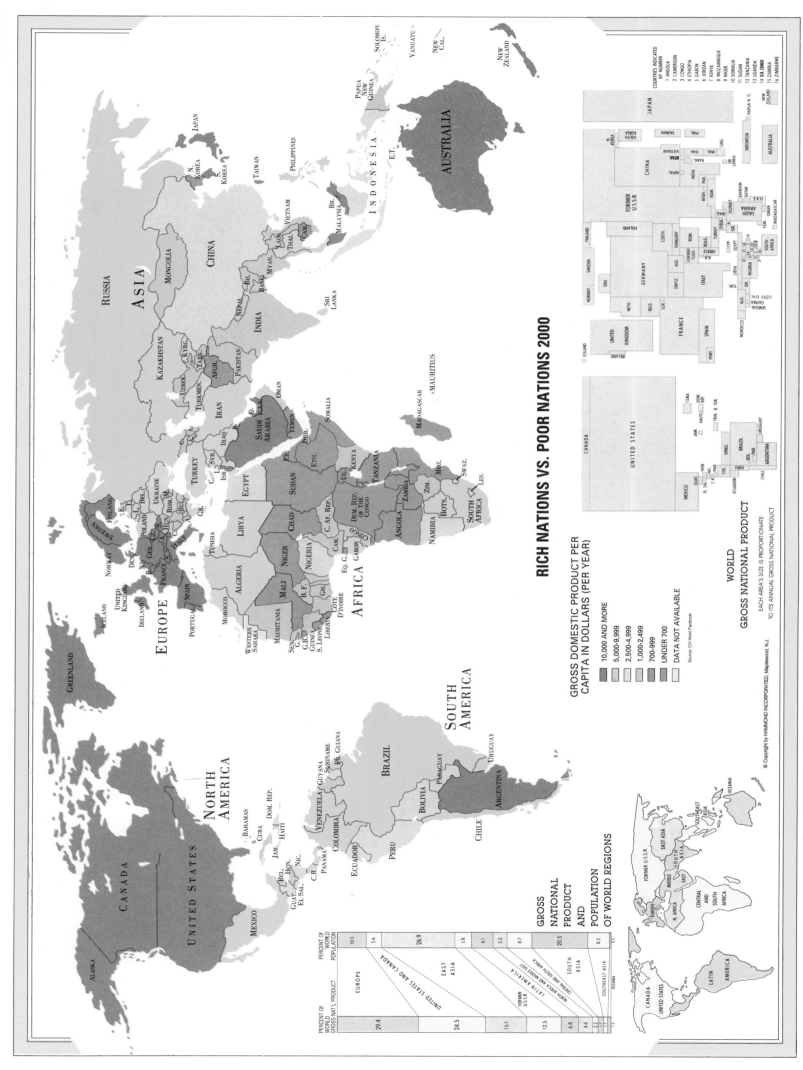

RICH NATIONS VS. POOR NATIONS 2000

GROSS DOMESTIC PRODUCT PER CAPITA IN DOLLARS (PER YEAR)

- 10,000 AND MORE
- 5,000-9,999
- 2,500-4,999
- 1,000-2,499
- 700-999
- UNDER 700
- DATA NOT AVAILABLE

Source: CIA World Factbook

WORLD GROSS NATIONAL PRODUCT

EACH AREA'S SIZE IS PROPORTIONATE TO ITS ANNUAL GROSS NATIONAL PRODUCT

© Copyright by HAMMOND INCORPORATED, Maplewood, N.J.

COUNTRIES INDICATED BY NUMBER
1 ANGOLA
2 CAMEROON
3 CONGO
4 ETHIOPIA
5 GABON
6 JORDAN
7 KENYA
8 MOZAMBIQUE
9 NIGER
10 SOMALIA
11 SUDAN
12 TANZANIA
13 UGANDA
14 DA. CONGO
15 ZAMBIA
16 ZIMBABWE

GROSS NATIONAL PRODUCT AND POPULATION OF WORLD REGIONS

PERCENT OF WORLD GROSS NAT'L PRODUCT		PERCENT OF WORLD POPULATION
29.4	EUROPE	10.5
		5.6
24.5	UNITED STATES AND CANADA	
	EAST ASIA	26.9
15.1	FORMER U.S.S.R.	5.8
12.5	LATIN AMERICA	8.1
6.8	NORTH AFRICA AND MIDDLE EAST	5.2
4.6	SOUTH ASIA	8.7
2.2	SOUTHEAST ASIA	20.5
1.7	OCEANIA	8.2
		0.5

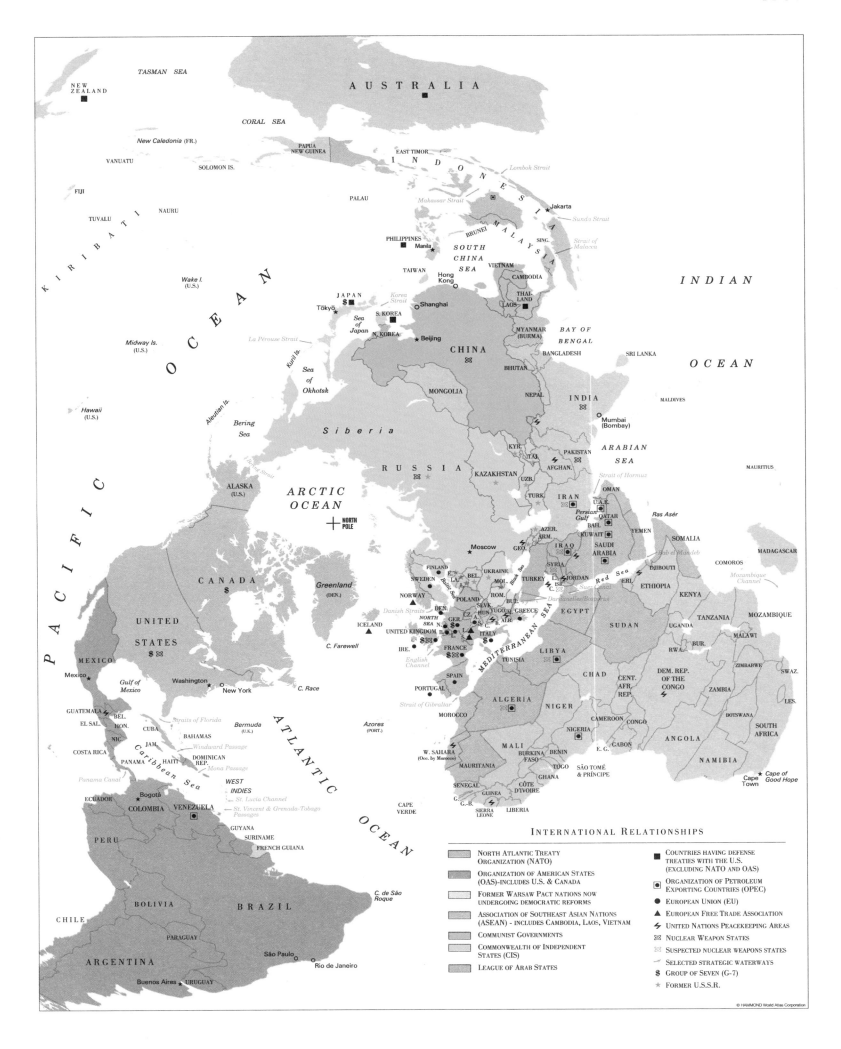

TASMAN SEA

NEW
ZEALAND

AUSTRALIA

CORAL SEA

New Caledonia (FR.)

PAPUA
NEW GUINEA

EAST TIMOR

INDONESIA

VANUATU

SOLOMON IS.

FIJI

KIRIBATI

TUVALU

NAURU

PALAU

Makassar Strait

Lombok Strait

Jakarta

Sunda Strait

PHILIPPINES   Manila

BRUNEI

MALAYSIA

SING.

Strait of Malacca

Wake I.
(U.S.)

SOUTH
CHINA
SEA

VIETNAM

CAMBODIA

INDIAN

TAIWAN

Hong Kong

THAI-
LAND

JAPAN

Korea
Strait

Shanghai

LAOS

MYANMAR
(BURMA)

BAY OF
BENGAL

OCEAN

Tōkyō

Sea of
Japan

S. KOREA

PACIFIC

Midway Is.
(U.S.)

La Pérouse Strait

N. KOREA

Beijing

CHINA

BANGLADESH

SRI LANKA

Kuril Is.

MONGOLIA

NEPAL

BHUTAN

INDIA

MALDIVES

Hawaii
(U.S.)

Sea of
Okhotsk

Siberia

KYR.

ARABIAN
SEA

Mumbai
(Bombay)

MAURITIUS

Aleutian Is.

Bering
Sea

RUSSIA

KAZAKHSTAN

TAJ.

AFGHAN.

PAKISTAN

Strait of Hormuz

OCEAN

ALASKA
(U.S.)

ARCTIC
OCEAN

UZB.

TURK.

IRAN

OMAN

U.A.E.

Ras Asér

Bering Strait

NORTH
POLE

Moscow

GEO.

AZER.
ARM.

Persian
Gulf

QATAR

BAH.

YEMEN

SOMALIA

CANADA

Greenland
(DEN.)

IRAQ

KUWAIT

SAUDI
ARABIA

Bab el Mandeb

MADAGASCAR

COMOROS

FINLAND

UKRAINE

SYRIA

Red Sea

DJIBOUTI

Mozambique
Channel

UNITED
STATES

SWEDEN

EST.
LAT.
LITH.

BEL.

MOL.

TURKEY

JORDAN

ISR.

ERI.

Suez Canal

ETHIOPIA

KENYA

NORWAY

POLAND

ROM.

BUL.

Black Sea

Dardanelles/Bosporus

EGYPT

SUDAN

UGANDA

TANZANIA

MEXICO

C. Farewell

DEN.

SLVK.
HUN.

GREECE

YUGO.

MEDITERRANEAN SEA

MOZAMBIQUE

Mexico

Gulf of
Mexico

ICELAND

NORTH
SEA

GER.

CZ.

A.

L. C.

ALB.

ITALY

MALAWI

Washington

New York

C. Race

UNITED KINGDOM

IRE.

LIBYA

LIBYA

RWA.

BUR.

ZIMBABWE

GUATEMALA

BEL.

FRANCE

English
Channel

TUNISIA

CHAD

CENT.
AFR.
REP.

DEM. REP.
OF THE
CONGO

ZAMBIA

SWAZ.

EL SAL.

HON.

Bermuda
(U.K.)

SPAIN

ALGERIA

NIGER

CONGO

ANGOLA

LES.

COSTA RICA

NIC.

CUBA

BAHAMAS

Azores
(PORT.)

PORTUGAL

MOROCCO

CAMEROON

GABON

NAMIBIA

SOUTH
AFRICA

JAM.

HAITI

DOMINICAN
REP.

Windward Passage

Mona Passage

Strait of Gibraltar

W. SAHARA
(Occ. by Morocco)

MALI

BURKINA
FASO

BENIN

NIGERIA

E. G.

SÃO TOMÉ
& PRÍNCIPE

Cape
Town

Cape of
Good Hope

Panama Canal

Caribbean Sea

WEST
INDIES

St. Lucia Channel

St. Vincent & Grenada-Tobago
Passages

CAPE
VERDE

MAURITANIA

SENEGAL

GUINEA

CÔTE
D'IVOIRE

GHANA

TOGO

ECUADOR

Bogotá

COLOMBIA

VENEZUELA

GUYANA

SURINAME

FRENCH GUIANA

G.

G.-B.

SIERRA
LEONE

LIBERIA

PERU

C. de São
Roque

BOLIVIA

BRAZIL

INTERNATIONAL RELATIONSHIPS

CHILE

PARAGUAY

São Paulo

Rio de Janeiro

NORTH ATLANTIC TREATY
ORGANIZATION (NATO)

COUNTRIES HAVING DEFENSE
TREATIES WITH THE U.S.
(EXCLUDING NATO AND OAS)

ARGENTINA

Buenos Aires

URUGUAY

ORGANIZATION OF AMERICAN STATES
(OAS)-INCLUDES U.S. & CANADA

ORGANIZATION OF PETROLEUM
EXPORTING COUNTRIES (OPEC)

FORMER WARSAW PACT NATIONS NOW
UNDERGOING DEMOCRATIC REFORMS

EUROPEAN UNION (EU)

ASSOCIATION OF SOUTHEAST ASIAN NATIONS
(ASEAN) - INCLUDES CAMBODIA, LAOS, VIETNAM

EUROPEAN FREE TRADE ASSOCIATION

UNITED NATIONS PEACEKEEPING AREAS

COMMUNIST GOVERNMENTS

NUCLEAR WEAPON STATES

COMMONWEALTH OF INDEPENDENT
STATES (CIS)

SUSPECTED NUCLEAR WEAPONS STATES

SELECTED STRATEGIC WATERWAYS

LEAGUE OF ARAB STATES

$ GROUP OF SEVEN (G-7)

★ FORMER U.S.S.R.

© HAMMOND World Atlas Corporation

TIME CHART

Well before 6000 B.C. people began to domesticate animals, and to gather and store grains and other crops in the Near East, Pakistan, the Americas, and China. Gradually, improved techniques of food production—the sowing of seed, cultivation and irrigation—were developed. Populations increased, trade in pottery and craft skills began, and new types of society and technology were possible.

The first use of copper metal occurred around 4000 B.C. in Anatolia and Iran.

DATE	NATIVE AMERICANS	BLACK AFRICANS	NORTH AFRICANS	EGYPTIANS	ARABIANS	IRANIANS	HEBREWS	PHOENICIANS	MESOPOTAMIANS	HITTITES	HELLENES (GREEKS)	AEGEANS
LATE STONE AGE	Clovis and Folsom big-game hunters in N. America											
	Manioc and high altitude grains in S. America		Mixed ancestral threads in Africa north of Sahara / Saharan pottery	Settled Egyptian communities in Nile Valley with Nubian, Saharan & Armenoid linkages					Extensive farming in Mesopotamia			
	Domestication of llama, alpaca in Andes		Nubian and S. African rock painting / Cattle domesticated						Earliest irrigation system c.5500			
5000 B.C.	Maize cultivated in Mexico								Early communities in the Tigris-Euphrates Valley			
				Badarian culture								
				Naqada I								
4000	First pottery in Americas		A-Group Nubian culture at Qustul	Predynasty Lower and Upper Kdms. / Naqada II					Growth of Sumerian cities			
	Cotton cultivated in Peru					Elamite civilization emerges			Cuneiform writing			
3000				Egyptian hieroglyphics / Menes unifies Egypt c. 2900		ELAM			1st dynasty of Ur		Migration of Greek-speaking peoples	
	Arctic Small Tool culture		Hunter-gatherers in West and Central Africa	OLD KDM. 2685-2180 / Pyramid Age				Phoenicians occupy coastal areas	Sargon I Akkadian dynasty		Aeolian & Achaean invasions	
2000 B.C.				1st Intermediate period		Wars with Babylon	Abraham	Extensive Mediterranean trade	BABYLONIA / ASSYRIA	Early Hittite Kingdoms		Palace at Knossos
1750				MIDDLE KDM. 2040-1786					OLD BABYLONIAN EMPIRE / Hammurabi c. 1700	Labarnas est. Empire c. 1700		Height of Cretan culture
				Hyksos invaders / 2nd Intermediate period					Mitanni Kdm.	HITTITE EMPIRE		MINOAN CIVILIZATION
1500	Early Pueblo culture in N. Amer. / First metalwork in Peru		Nubia invaded by Eygpt	NEW KINGDOM 1570-1070 / Thutmose III / Ikhnaton				Egyptian rule	Kassite rule / Iron weapons introduced		Mycenae / Ionian invasion	Fall of Crete 1400
1250	Olmec civilization 1200-900			Invasion of Sea Peoples / Rameses II / 3rd Intermediate period 1070-712			Exodus c. 1290 / Conquest of Canaan		Shalman-eser I / Battle of Kadesh 1296		Trojan War c. 1190	
			Utica founded by Phoenicians						Tiglath-pileser I	Hittites driven from Asia Minor	Dorian invasion	
1000 B.C.	Mayas enter Cent. Amer.		Libyan dynasty	EGYPT	Minaean Kdm.	Golden Age of Elam	David / Solomon	Hiram of Tyre	Aramaean invasion		Local aristocracies	

HITTITE KDM.

ASSYRIA

BABYLONIAN EMP.

EGYPTIAN KDM.

ANCIENT EMPIRES
—— Assyrian Empire 7th Cent. B.C.

A Graphic History of Mankind

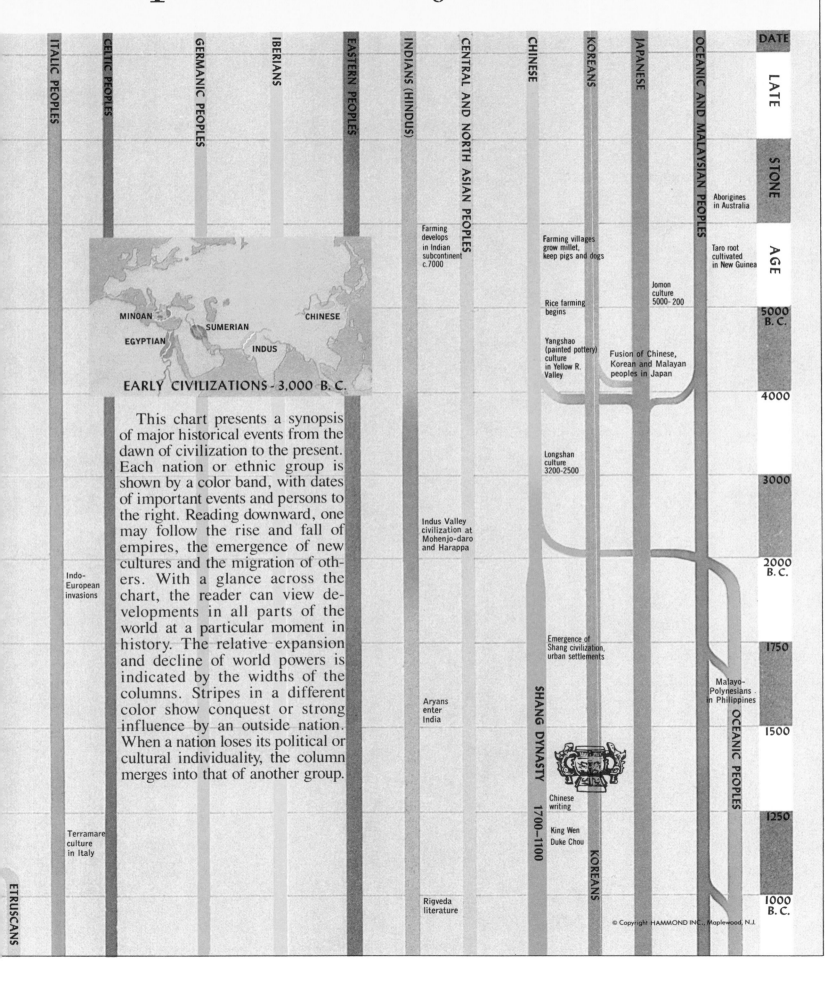

EARLY CIVILIZATIONS - 3,000 B.C.

MINOAN

SUMERIAN

CHINESE

EGYPTIAN

INDUS

This chart presents a synopsis of major historical events from the dawn of civilization to the present. Each nation or ethnic group is shown by a color band, with dates of important events and persons to the right. Reading downward, one may follow the rise and fall of empires, the emergence of new cultures and the migration of others. With a glance across the chart, the reader can view developments in all parts of the world at a particular moment in history. The relative expansion and decline of world powers is indicated by the widths of the columns. Stripes in a different color show conquest or strong influence by an outside nation. When a nation loses its political or cultural individuality, the column merges into that of another group.

ITALIC PEOPLES

CELTIC PEOPLES

GERMANIC PEOPLES

IBERIANS

EASTERN PEOPLES

INDIANS (HINDUS)

CENTRAL AND NORTH ASIAN PEOPLES

CHINESE

KOREANS

JAPANESE

OCEANIC AND MALAYSIAN PEOPLES

DATE

LATE

STONE

AGE

Indo-European invasions

Terramare culture in Italy

ETRUSCANS

Farming develops in Indian subcontinent c.7000

Indus Valley civilization at Mohenjo-daro and Harappa

Aryans enter India

Rigveda literature

Farming villages grow millet, keep pigs and dogs

Rice farming begins

Yangshao (painted pottery) culture in Yellow R. Valley

Longshan culture 3200-2500

Emergence of Shang civilization, urban settlements

SHANG DYNASTY 1700-1100

Chinese writing

King Wen Duke Chou

Jomon culture 5000-200

Fusion of Chinese, Korean and Malayan peoples in Japan

KOREANS

Aborigines in Australia

Taro root cultivated in New Guinea

Malayo-Polynesians in Philippines

OCEANIC PEOPLES

5000 B.C.

4000

3000

2000 B.C.

1750

1500

1250

1000 B.C.

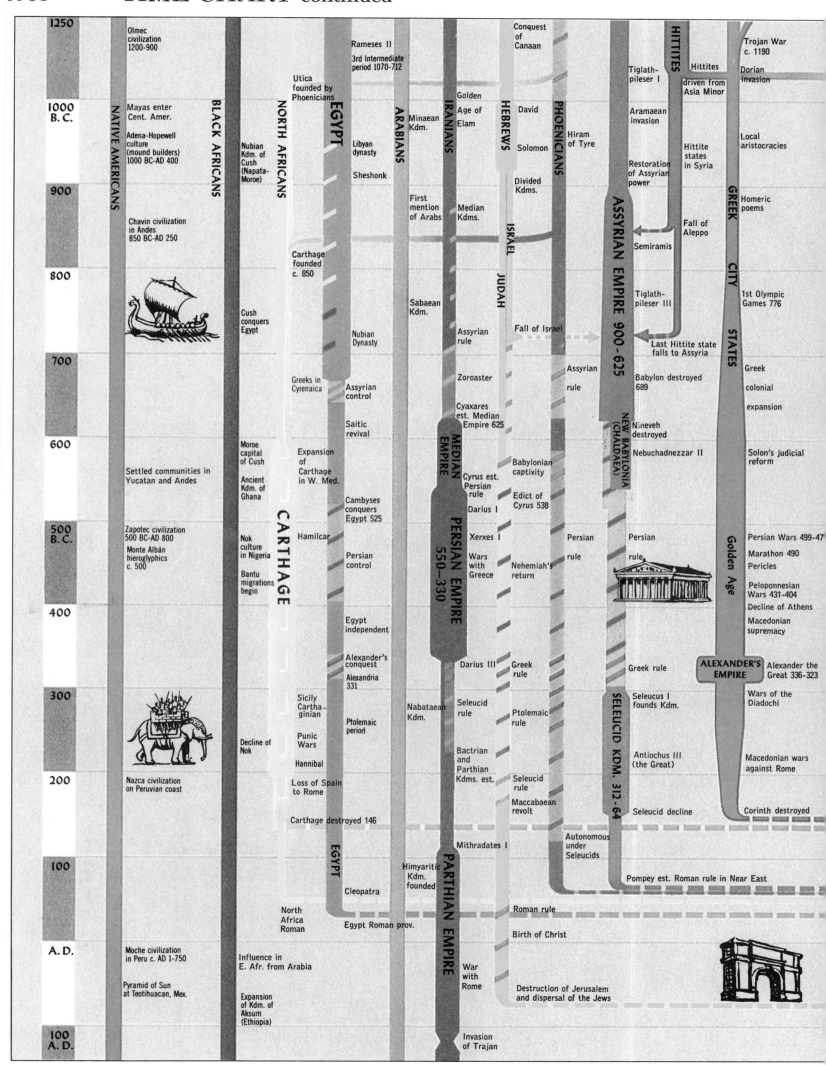

Time scale (left axis): 1250, 1000 B.C., 900, 800, 700, 600, 500 B.C., 400, 300, 200, 100, A.D., 100 A.D.

NATIVE AMERICANS
- Olmec civilization 1200–900
- Mayas enter Cent. Amer.
- Adena-Hopewell culture (mound builders) 1000 BC–AD 400
- Chavin civilization in Andes 850 BC–AD 250
- Settled communities in Yucatan and Andes
- Zapotec civilization 500 BC–AD 800
- Monte Albán hieroglyphics c. 500
- Nazca civilization on Peruvian coast
- Moche civilization in Peru c. AD 1–750
- Pyramid of Sun at Teotihuacan, Mex.

BLACK AFRICANS
- Nubian Kdm. of Cush (Napata-Moroe)
- Cush conquers Egypt
- Moroe capital of Cush
- Ancient Kdm. of Ghana
- Nok culture in Nigeria
- Bantu migrations begin
- Decline of Nok
- Influence in E. Afr. from Arabia
- Expansion of Kdm. of Aksum (Ethiopia)

NORTH AFRICANS / CARTHAGE
- Utica founded by Phoenicians
- Carthage founded c. 850
- Greeks in Cyrenaica
- Expansion of Carthage in W. Med.
- Hamilcar
- Sicily Carthaginian
- Punic Wars
- Hannibal
- Loss of Spain to Rome
- Carthage destroyed 146
- North Africa Roman

EGYPT
- Rameses II
- 3rd Intermediate period 1070–712
- Libyan dynasty
- Sheshonk
- Nubian Dynasty
- Saitic revival
- Cambyses conquers Egypt 525
- Persian control
- Egypt independent
- Alexander's conquest
- Alexandria 331
- Ptolemaic period
- Cleopatra
- Egypt Roman prov.

ARABIANS
- Minaean Kdm.
- First mention of Arabs
- Sabaean Kdm.
- Nabataean Kdm.
- Himyaritic Kdm. founded

IRANIANS / MEDIAN EMPIRE / PERSIAN EMPIRE 550–330 / PARTHIAN EMPIRE
- Golden Age of Elam
- Median Kdms.
- Assyrian rule
- Zoroaster
- Cyaxares est. Median Empire 625
- Cyrus est. Persian rule
- Darius I
- Xerxes I
- Wars with Greece
- Darius III
- Seleucid rule
- Bactrian and Parthian Kdms. est.
- Mithradates I
- War with Rome
- Invasion of Trajan

HEBREWS / ISRAEL / JUDAH
- Conquest of Canaan
- David
- Solomon
- Divided Kdms.
- Fall of Israel
- Babylonian captivity
- Edict of Cyrus 538
- Nehemiah's return
- Greek rule
- Seleucid rule
- Maccabaean revolt
- Birth of Christ
- Destruction of Jerusalem and dispersal of the Jews

PHOENICIANS
- Hiram of Tyre
- Assyrian rule
- Persian rule
- Ptolemaic rule
- Roman rule

ASSYRIAN EMPIRE 900–625 / NEW BABYLONIA (CHALDAEA) / SELEUCID KDM. 312–64
- Tiglath-pileser I
- Aramaean invasion
- Restoration of Assyrian power
- Semiramis
- Tiglath-pileser III
- Babylon destroyed 689
- Nineveh destroyed
- Nebuchadnezzar II
- Persian rule
- Greek rule
- Seleucus I founds Kdm.
- Antiochus III (the Great)
- Seleucid decline
- Autonomous under Seleucids
- Pompey est. Roman rule in Near East

HITTITES
- Hittites driven from Asia Minor
- Hittite states in Syria
- Fall of Aleppo
- Last Hittite state falls to Assyria

GREEK CITY STATES / Golden Age / ALEXANDER'S EMPIRE
- Trojan War c. 1190
- Dorian invasion
- Local aristocracies
- Homeric poems
- 1st Olympic Games 776
- Greek colonial expansion
- Solon's judicial reform
- Persian Wars 499–47
- Marathon 490
- Pericles
- Peloponnesian Wars 431–404
- Decline of Athens
- Macedonian supremacy
- Alexander the Great 336–323
- Wars of the Diadochi
- Macedonian wars against Rome
- Corinth destroyed

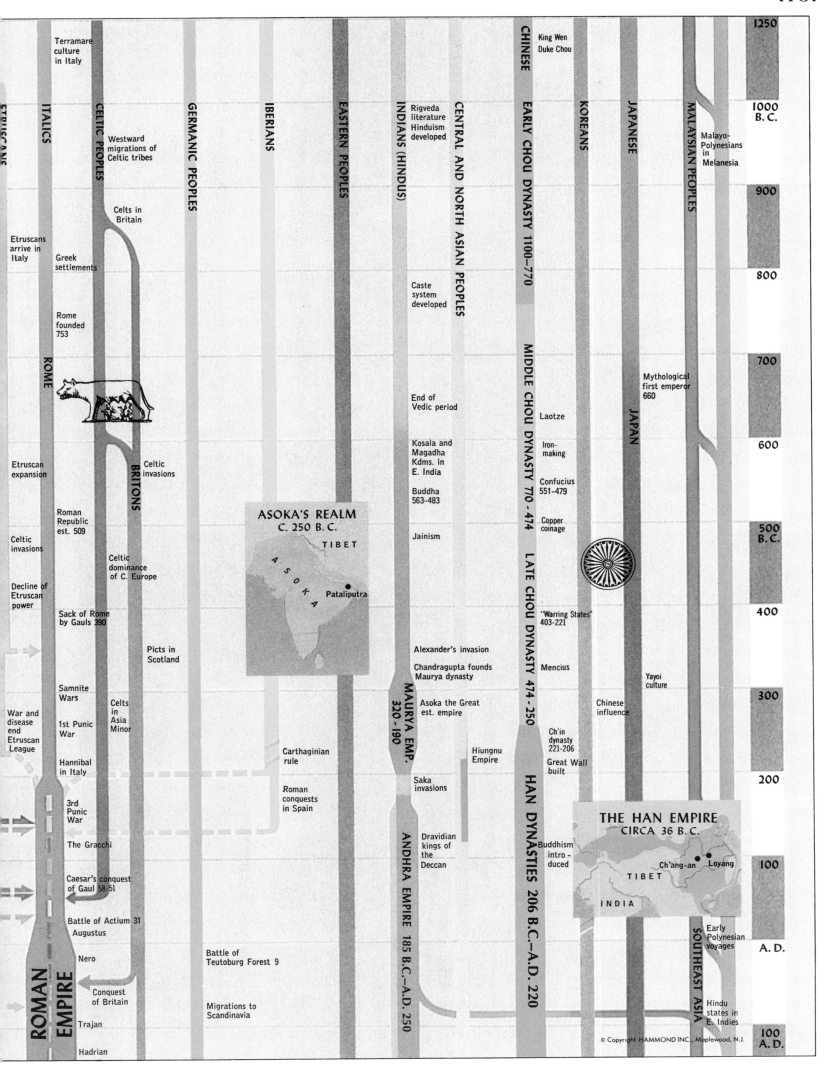

ETRUSCANS

ITALICS

Terramare
culture
in Italy

Etruscans
arrive in
Italy

Greek
settlements

Rome
founded
753

ROME

Etruscan
expansion

Roman
Republic
est. 509

Celtic
invasions

Decline of
Etruscan
power

Sack of Rome
by Gauls 390

War and
disease
end
Etruscan
League

Samnite
Wars

1st Punic
War

Hannibal
in Italy

3rd
Punic
War

The Gracchi

Caesar's conquest
of Gaul 58-51

Battle of Actium 31
Augustus

ROMAN EMPIRE

Nero

Conquest
of Britain

Trajan

Hadrian

CELTIC PEOPLES

Westward
migrations of
Celtic tribes

Celts in
Britain

BRITONS

Celtic
invasions

Celtic
dominance
of C. Europe

Picts in
Scotland

Celts
in
Asia
Minor

GERMANIC PEOPLES

Battle of
Teutoburg Forest 9

Migrations to
Scandinavia

IBERIANS

Carthaginian
rule

Roman
conquests
in Spain

EASTERN PEOPLES

ASOKA'S REALM C. 250 B.C.

TIBET

ASOKA

Pataliputra

INDIANS (HINDUS)

Rigveda
literature
Hinduism
developed

Caste
system
developed

End of
Vedic period

Kosala and
Magadha
Kdms. in
E. India

Buddha
563-483

Jainism

Alexander's invasion

Chandragupta founds
Maurya dynasty

Asoka the Great
est. empire

MAURYA EMP. 320 - 190

Saka
invasions

Dravidian
kings of
the
Deccan

ANDHRA EMPIRE 185 B.C.–A.D. 250

CENTRAL AND NORTH ASIAN PEOPLES

Hiungnu
Empire

CHINESE

King Wen
Duke Chou

EARLY CHOU DYNASTY 1100–770

MIDDLE CHOU DYNASTY 770 - 474

Laotze

Iron-
making

Confucius
551-479

Copper
coinage

LATE CHOU DYNASTY 474 - 250

"Warring States"
403-221

Mencius

Ch'in
dynasty
221-206

Great Wall
built

HAN DYNASTIES 206 B.C.—A.D. 220

Buddhism
intro -
duced

THE HAN EMPIRE CIRCA 36 B.C.

Ch'ang-an   Loyang

TIBET

INDIA

KOREANS

JAPANESE

JAPAN

Mythological
first emperor
660

Yayoi
culture

Chinese
influence

MALAYSIAN PEOPLES

Malayo-
Polynesians
in Melanesia

SOUTHEAST ASIA

Early
Polynesian
voyages

Hindu
states in
E. Indies

1250

1000
B. C.

900

800

700

600

500
B. C.

400

300

200

100

A. D.

100
A.D.

© Copyright HAMMOND INC., Maplewood, N.J.

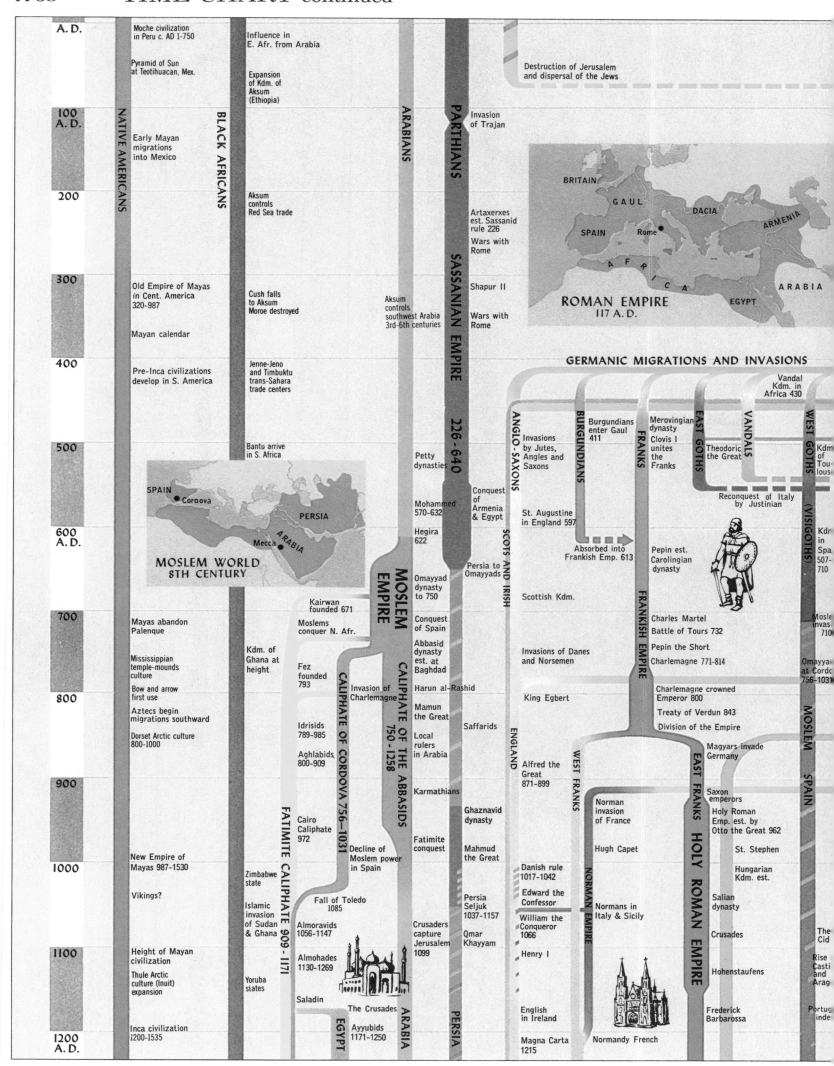

A.D.

100 A.D.

200

300

400

500

600 A.D.

700

800

900

1000

1100

1200 A.D.

NATIVE AMERICANS

Moche civilization in Peru c. AD 1-750

Pyramid of Sun at Teotihuacan, Mex.

Early Mayan migrations into Mexico

Old Empire of Mayas in Cent. America 320-987

Mayan calendar

Pre-Inca civilizations develop in S. America

Mayas abandon Palenque

Mississippian temple-mounds culture

Bow and arrow first use

Aztecs begin migrations southward

Dorset Arctic culture 800-1000

New Empire of Mayas 987-1530

Vikings?

Height of Mayan civilization

Thule Arctic culture (Inuit) expansion

Inca civilization 1200-1535

BLACK AFRICANS

Influence in E. Afr. from Arabia

Expansion of Kdm. of Aksum (Ethiopia)

Aksum controls Red Sea trade

Cush falls to Aksum Moroe destroyed

Jenne-Jeno and Timbuktu trans-Sahara trade centers

Bantu arrive in S. Africa

Kdm. of Ghana at height

Zimbabwe state

Islamic invasion of Sudan & Ghana

Yoruba states

ARABIANS

Aksum controls southwest Arabia 3rd-6th centuries

SPAIN
Cordova
PERSIA
ARABIA
Mecca
MOSLEM WORLD 8TH CENTURY

Kairwan founded 671

Moslems conquer N. Afr.

Fez founded 793

Idrisids 789-985

Aghlabids 800-909

Cairo Caliphate 972

FATIMITE CALIPHATE 909-1171

Almoravids 1056-1147

Almohades 1130-1269

Saladin

EGYPT

Ayyubids 1171-1250

CALIPHATE OF CORDOVA 756-1031

Invasion of Charlemagne

MOSLEM EMPIRE

CALIPHATE OF THE ABBASIDS 750-1258

Petty dynasties

Mohammed 570-632

Hegira 622

Omayyad dynasty to 750

Conquest of Spain

Abbasid dynasty est. at Baghdad

Harun al-Rashid

Mamun the Great

Local rulers in Arabia

Karmathians

Ghaznavid dynasty

Fatimite conquest

Decline of Moslem power in Spain

Fall of Toledo 1085

Crusaders capture Jerusalem 1099

The Crusades

ARABIA

PARTHIANS

SASSANIAN EMPIRE 226-640

Invasion of Trajan

Artaxerxes est. Sassanid rule 226

Wars with Rome

Shapur II

Wars with Rome

Conquest of Armenia & Egypt

Persia to Omayyads

Saffarids

Persia Seljuk 1037-1157

Qmar Khayyam

PERSIA

Destruction of Jerusalem and dispersal of the Jews

BRITAIN
GAUL
DACIA
ARMENIA
SPAIN
Rome
AFRICA
ARABIA
EGYPT
ROMAN EMPIRE 117 A.D.

GERMANIC MIGRATIONS AND INVASIONS

Vandal Kdm. in Africa 430

ANGLO-SAXONS

Invasions by Jutes, Angles and Saxons

St. Augustine in England 597

SCOTS AND IRISH

Scottish Kdm.

ENGLAND

King Egbert

Alfred the Great 871-899

Danish rule 1017-1042

Edward the Confessor

William the Conqueror 1066

Henry I

English in Ireland

Magna Carta 1215

BURGUNDIANS

Burgundians enter Gaul 411

Absorbed into Frankish Emp. 613

FRANKS

Merovingian dynasty

Clovis I unites the Franks

FRANKISH EMPIRE

Pepin est. Carolingian dynasty

Charles Martel

Battle of Tours 732

Pepin the Short

Charlemagne 771-814

Charlemagne crowned Emperor 800

Treaty of Verdun 843

Division of the Empire

WEST FRANKS

Norman invasion of France

Hugh Capet

NORMAN EMPIRE

Normans in Italy & Sicily

Normandy French

EAST GOTHS

Theodoric the Great

Reconquest of Italy by Justinian

VANDALS

EAST FRANKS

Magyars invade Germany

Saxon emperors

Holy Roman Emp. est. by Otto the Great 962

St. Stephen

Hungarian Kdm. est.

Salian dynasty

Crusades

HOLY ROMAN EMPIRE

Hohenstaufens

Frederick Barbarossa

WEST GOTHS (VISIGOTHS)

Kdm of Toulouse

Kdm in Spa 507-710

Mosle invas 710

Omayya at Cordo 756-1031

MOSLEM SPAIN

The Cid

Rise Casti and Arag

Portug inde

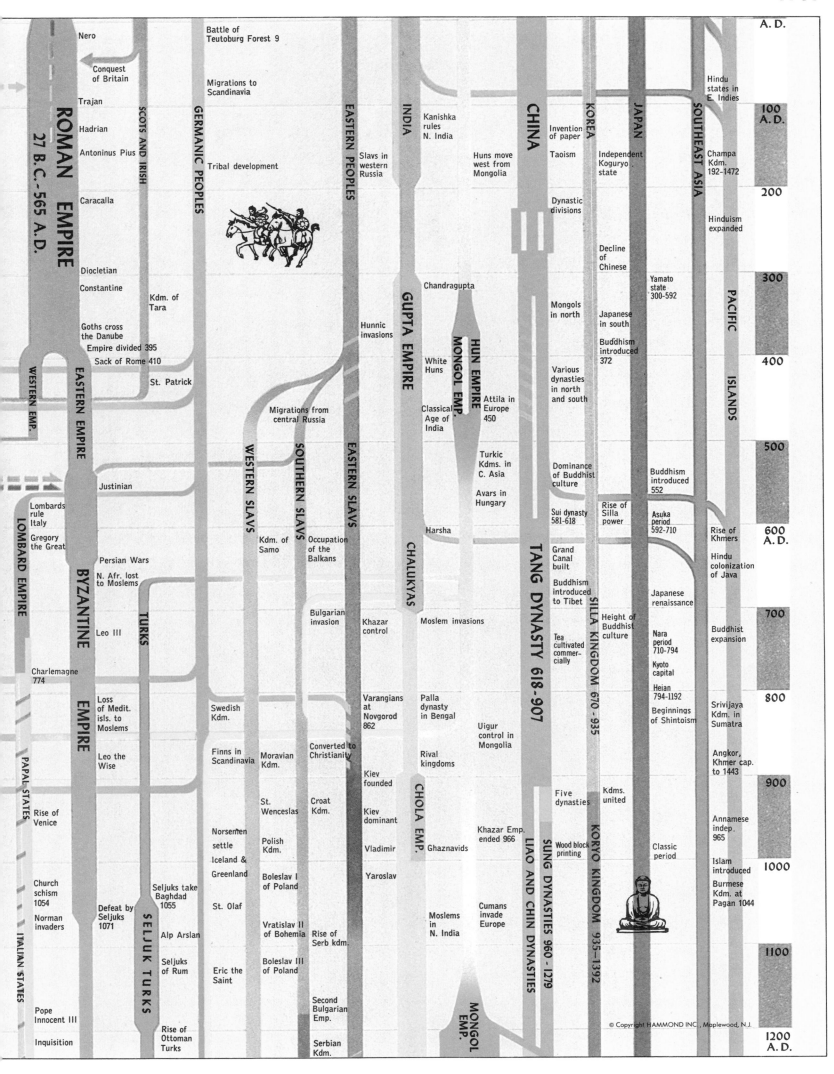

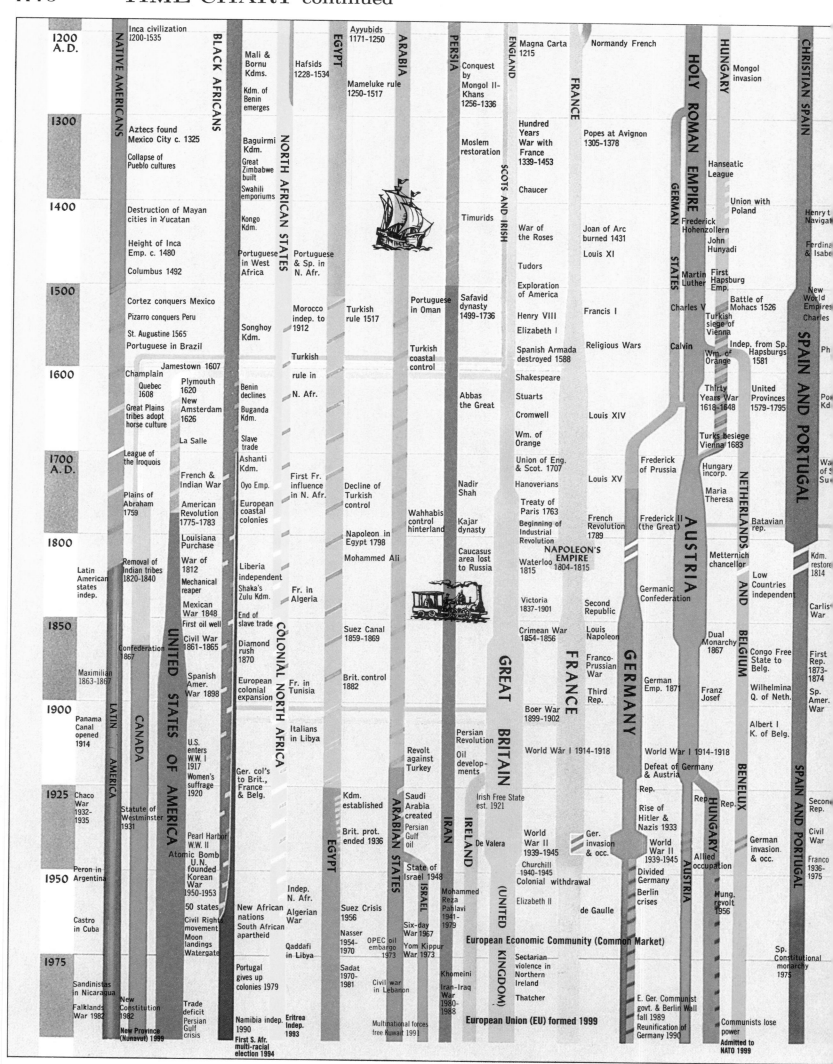

Time scale (right edge): 1200 A.D. · 1300 · 1400 · 1500 · 1600 · 1700 A.D. · 1800 · 1850 · 1900 · 1925 · 1950 · 1975

ITALIAN STATES / ITALY
- Inquisition
- Rise of Genoa
- Dante
- Height of Venetian sea power
- Great Schism 1378-1417
- Medici
- da Vinci
- Andrea Doria
- Michelangelo
- Galileo
- ssion
- Napoleon's conquests
- Mazzini
- War of indep.
- Garibaldi
- Cavour unifies Italy 1861
- Kdm. of Italy 1870
- Italo-Turkish War 1911-1912
- Mussolini comes to power 1922
- Abyssinia attacked 1935
- World War II
- Rep.

BYZANTINE GREEKS / GREECE
- Crusaders take Constantinople 1204
- Palaeologi 1261-1453
- Turks take Constantinople 1453
- Greek War of indep. 1821-1830
- Otto I
- George I
- Modern Olympic Games 1896
- Balkan Wars
- Republic
- Kdm. restored 1935
- Civil War 1944-1950
- Military dictatorship 1967-1974 Republic 1975

OTTOMAN EMPIRE 1299-1923 / TURKEY
- Rise of Ottoman Turks
- Mohammed I
- Mohammed the Conqueror
- Suleiman the Magnificent
- Battle of Lepanto 1571
- Vienna besieged 1683
- Russo-Turkish wars
- Battle of Navarino 1827
- Russo-Turkish War 1877
- Young Turk movement
- World War I
- Atatürk forms rep.
- German invasion & occ.
- Turks invade Cyprus 1974
- Kurdish Conflict 1993

SCANDINAVIA
- Union of Kalmar
- Finland to Sweden
- Gustavus Adolphus
- Charles XII
- Finland to Russia 1809
- Norway separate
- Finland indep. 1918
- German occ. of Denmark & Norway

WESTERN SLAVS
- Hussite Wars
- Poland and Lithuania united
- Hapsburgs in Bohemia
- John Sobieski
- Bohemia to Austria
- Polish partitions
- Polish Kdm. under Russia
- First Polish Revolution
- Second Polish Revolution
- Pilsudski
- Slavic states independent
- German control of Poland & Czech.
- Holocaust Soviet satellites
- Soviets invade Czechoslovakia 1968
- Polish Solidarity movement
- Communists lose power in E. Europe 1989
- Poland admitted to NATO 1999

SOUTHERN SLAVS
- Serbian Kdm.
- Turkish control of Balkans
- Livonian War
- Austrian invasion
- Serb uprising
- Balkans auton.
- Bulgaria & Serbia indep.
- Balkan Wars
- German control in Balkans
- Tito in Yugoslavia 1945-1980
- Breakup of Yugoslavia, 1992 Czech Rep. 1993
- Kosovo Conflict 1999

EASTERN SLAVS / RUSSIAN EMPIRE / SOVIET UNION
- Kievan Rus era ends
- End of Mongol control
- Ivan the Great
- Ivan the Terrible
- Romanov dynasty 1613-1917
- Peter the Great
- Catharine the Great
- Napoleon's invasion
- Crimean War 1854-1856
- Central Asian expansion
- Russo-Japanese War 1904-1905
- World War I
- Russian Revolution 1917
- U.S.S.R. formed 1922
- Stalin 1926-1953
- World War II German invasion
- Cold War with West
- Sputnik 1957
- Soviet occupation of Afghanistan 1979-1989
- Breakup of Soviet Union 1991

INDIA / MOGUL EMPIRE / SOUTH ASIAN NATIONS
- Sult. of Delhi
- Vasco da Gama at Calicut 1498
- Sikh religion founded
- Akbar the Great
- East India Company 1600
- Aurangzeb 1658-1707
- Clive 1725-1774
- Afghan war
- Sepoy Rebellion 1857
- Gold strikes
- World War I
- Gandhi's passive resistance 1920's-1948
- World War II
- Indep. of India, Pakistan & Ceylon (Sri Lanka)
- Border clash with China 1962
- Bangladesh 1971
- Sikh separatism
- Kashmir Conflict 1999

MONGOL EMPIRE / KHANATE OF THE GOLDEN HORDE / TATAR EMPIRE 1368-1409
- Genghis Khan 1206-1227
- JAGATAI
- Timur sacks Delhi
- Timur (Tamerlane)
- Volga Khanates lost to Russia
- Manchu conquest
- British convicts to Australia 1788
- Aborigines move inland
- New Zealand colonized 1840
- N.Z.-Maori wars
- Dominion status to Austr. & N.Z.
- World War I
- World War II
- ANZUS Treaty 1951
- Aborigines gain vote
- N.Z. bans nuclear ships & weapons

EMPIRE OF GENGHIS KHAN (map: ARABIA · PERSIA · TURKESTAN · MONGOLIA · TIBET · INDIA)

YÜAN DYNASTY 1260-1368 / MING DYNASTY 1368-1644 / MANCHU (CH'ING) DYNASTY 1644-1912 / CHINA
- Chu Shi Neo-Confucianism
- Genghis Khan 1206-1227
- Kublai Khan
- Marco Polo in China
- Growth of Moslems
- Christian missionaries
- Portuguese in Canton & Macao
- Manchu occupation 1637
- Tibet conquered 1750
- Opium wars
- Taiping Rebellion 1850-1864
- Sino-Japanese War 1894-1895
- Boxer Rebellion 1900
- Sun Yat-sen, Rep. 1912
- Manchukuo Japanese
- Communist China 1948
- Mao Tse-tung Cultural Revolution
- Border clashes with U.S.S.R.
- U.S. recognizes Communist China 1979
- Economic reforms
- Pro-democracy protests crushed 1989
- Hong Kong to China 1997

KOREA
- Mongol invasions
- Korean renaissance
- Yi dynasty (to 20th century)
- Korea opened to West 1876
- Annexed by Japan 1910
- Divided Korea
- Korean War 1950-1953

JAPAN / ASHIKAGA SHOGUNATE 1333-1573 / TOKUGAWA SHOGUNATE 1600-1868 / JAPANESE EMPIRE
- Feudal Kamakura period 1192-1333
- Mongol invasions
- Civil wars
- Rise of the shoguns
- Onin War
- First Portuguese visit
- St. Francis Xavier Edo 1603-1867
- Tokyo capital
- Christianity introduced
- Decline of Shogunate
- Perry's visit 1854
- Meiji Restoration 1868-1912
- Russo-Japanese War 1904-1905
- World War I 1914
- Hirohito (Showa) 1926-1989
- World War II
- Economic prosperity
- Government scandals
- Akihito

SOUTHEAST ASIA / PACIFIC ISLANDS / S.E. ASIAN STATES
- Thai migrations
- Maoris to N.Z.
- Thai Kdm. at Ayutthaya 1350-1767
- Decline of Khmers
- Fall of Madjapahit Kdm. in Java
- Burma united
- Magellan 1521
- Dutch found Batavia 1619
- Captain James Cook
- Thai Kdm. at Bangkok
- Raffles founds Singapore 1819
- French & Brit. protectorates
- World War I
- World War II
- Fr.-Indochina War
- Indep. of S. E. Asian States
- Vietnam Conflict 1959-1975
- New Pacific nations

© Copyright HAMMOND INC., Maplewood, N.J.

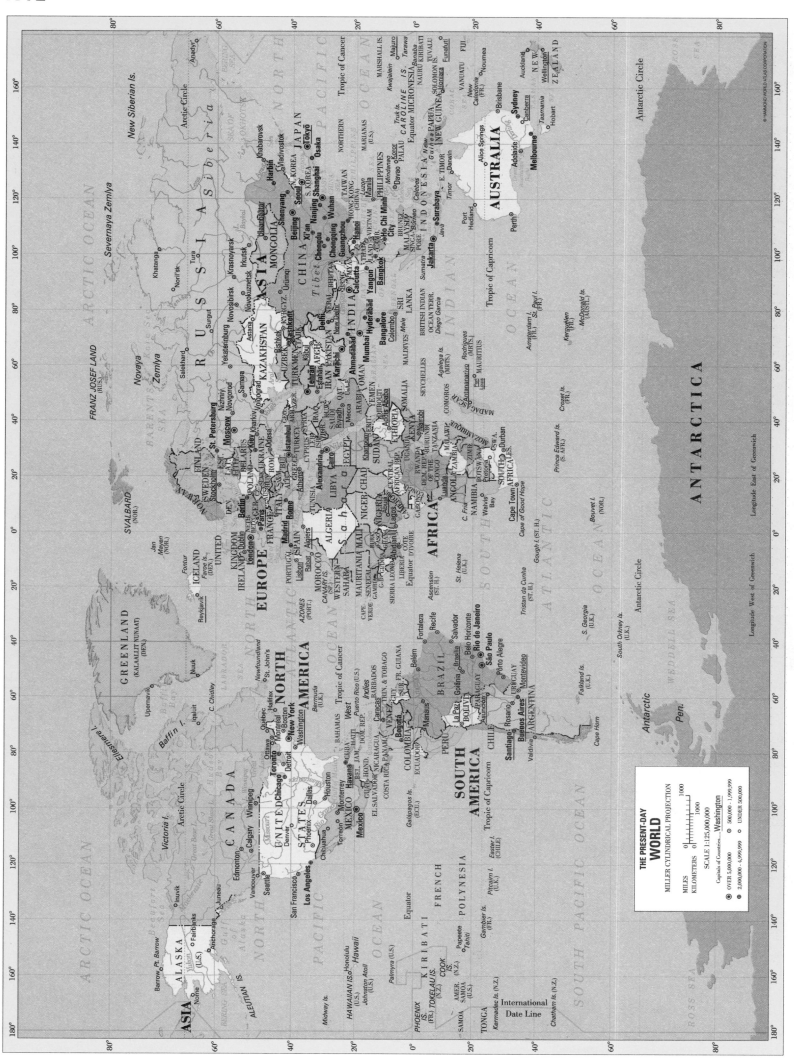

THE PRESENT-DAY
WORLD
MILLER CYLINDRICAL PROJECTION

SCALE 1:125,000,000

MILES
KILOMETERS

Capitals of Countries.......Washington

⊛ OVER 5,000,000   ⊙ 500,000 - 1,999,999
⊕ 2,000,000 - 4,999,999   ○ UNDER 500,000

INDEX

	Index Ref.	Plate No.
Abbasids, Caliphate of the	C-2	H18
Abo	J-6	H38
Abyssinia (Ethiopia) (left)	F-6	H41
Acadia	M-9	H26
Acarnania (bottom)	B-2	H 6
Achaia, (bottom)	B,C-2	H 6
Achaia, Princ. of	F-5	H19
Acre (bottom inset)		H17
Acropolis (bottom)	A-3	H 6
Actium (bottom)	B-2	H 6
Adae	Map 13	VII
Adalia (bottom)	E-2	H37
Adana (bottom)	E-2	H37
Aden	G-7	H54
Admiralty Is. (bottom)	E-4	H50
Adowa (left)	F-5	H41
Adrianople (top)	D-1	H37
Aegean Sea		H 6
Aegina (bottom)	C-3	H 6
Aeolis (bottom)	E-2	H 6
Aetolia (bottom)	B-2	H 6
Afghanistan	K-3	H54
Africa (Roman prov.)	K-7	H 8
Agadir (left)	A-3	H41
Agincourt	W-20	H22
Aiguesmortes (bottom)	A-2	H17
Aigun	F-7	H38
Aix-la-Chapelle	E-2	H13
Ajanta (bottom)	E-3	H10
Akkad	C-3	H 4
Akyab (bottom)	B-3	H50
Alamanni	D-3	H11
Alans	L-3,A-4	H11
Alaska Highway	H-2	H49
Albania	G-4	H44
Albi	D-6	H22
Alcazar (El Ksar el Kebir)	A-7	H24
Alemania	E-3	H13
Aleutian Is. (bottom)	G-1	H50
Alexander's Empire		H 8
Alexandretta (bottom)	E-2	H37
Alexandria	B-2	H 7
Algeciras	D-5	H44
Algeria	B-2	H57
Algiers (left)	C-3	H41
Almería (top)	B-4	H48
Almohad Caliphate	Map 10	V
Almohades, Dominions of the	D-5	H19
Almoravids, Dominions of the (top)	B-3	H17
Alsace & Lorraine	B-3	H35
Amalfi (top)	E-2	H17
Amberg (left)	E-4	H30
Amiens	K-5	H45
Amoy (bottom)	D-4	H48
Amur District	F-6	H38
Anasazi	Map 8	IV
Anatolia	E-2	H37
Anbar (bottom)	G-3	H15
Andhra (top)	E-4	H10
Andorra	C-5	H27
Andrussof	D-3	H28
Angevin Empire		H22
Angkor	F-3	H18
Angles	D-2	H11
Angola	B-4	H57
Angora (Ankara)	E-1	H37
Anjou	O-16	H22
Antioch (bottom inset)		H17
Antonine Wall	B-2	H14
Anuradhapura	F-4	H10
Anzio (top)	E-3	H50
Apache	Map 11	VI
Aquae Sils (Bath)	C-4	H14
Aquileia	D-2	H 9
Aquitaine	D-3	H13
Arabia	C-2	H18
Arabs	Map 7	IV
Aragon	D-4	H19
Arawak	Map 10	V
Arbela	D-2	H 8
Arcadia (bottom)	C-3	H 6
Arelate	L-4	H13
Argentina (right)		H33
Argonne Forest	L-5	H45
Argos (bottom)	C-3	H 6
Armenia	C-2	H 7
Arras	K-4	H45
Artois	Q-14	H22
Aryans	C-3	H 7
Asad (top)	G-4	H15
Asante	E-8	H40
Ascalon (bottom inset)		H17
Ashdod (top)	D-4	H 6
Asia (Roman prov.)	M-7	H 8
Asia Minor	F-3	H15
Asir (right)	D-5	H41
Askikaga Japan	Map 12	VI
Asoka's Empire	D-2	H 7
Aspromonte	F-5	H34
Assab	R-18	H40
Assassins (bottom inset)		H17
Assyria (top)	F-2	H 5
Astrakhan, Khanate of	F-3	H38
Athens (bottom)	A-3	H 6
Athens, Duchy of	F-5	H19
Attica (bottom)	C-3	H 6
Attu (bottom)	F-1	H50
Augsburg	E-4	H19
Auschwitz (top)	E-3	H50
Ausculum	E-4	H 9
Austerlitz	J-4	H31
Australia		H42
Australasia	E-2	H13
Austria	F-4	H46
Austria-Hungary	F-4	H44
Austrian Netherlands	G-3	H26
Auvergne	Q-17	H22
Avar Kingdom	E-3	H12
Avignon	C-5	H25
Axis Powers		H49
Axum	G-8	H40
Axumite Kingdom (bottom)	C-4	H10
Ayacucho (right)	F-1	H33
Ayyubids, Sultanate of the (bottom)	H-4	H17
Azd (top)	G-5	H15
Azerbaijan	G-1	H54
Azores	N-4	H49
Azov	F-1	H37
Aztec Empire	Map D	H 3
Babylon (bottom)	D-2	H 5
Babylonia	G-3	H 4
Babylonian Empire		H 5
Bactrian Kdm	D-2	H 7
Badajoz (top)	B-4	H48
Baden (top)	C-3	H35
Badr (Bedr) (top)	F-4	H15
Baghdad	M-6	H13
Bagirmi (left)	D-5	H41
Bagtiginids	H-4	H19
Bahia (left)		H33
Bakr (top)	G-4	H15
Balaklava	A-5	H38
Balearic Is. (bottom)	A-3	H17
Balkh (bottom)	J-3	H15
Banat	L-4	H26
Bandung	R-6	H59
Bangladesh	C-4	H55
Bantu	B-3	H40
Bar	H-8	H28
Bar, Duchy of	R-15	H22
Barbary States	K-3	H23
Barca (bottom)	E-3	H15
Barcelona	C-3	H16
Bardo (bottom)	B-2	H37
Bari (top)	F-2	H17
Barotseland (left)	E-8	H41
Basel (left)	D-4	H30
Basques	B-3	H12
Basra	G-3	H15
Bastarnae	M-6	H 8
Bastille (bottom)	D-3	H29
Bataan Peninsula (bottom)	C-3	H50
Batavia (right)	G-6	H41
Batavian Rep. (left)	D-3	H30
Batum	A-6	H38
Bavaria (top)	C-3	H35
Bavarians	D-3	H12
Belém (Para)		H33
Belgium (top)	B-2	H35
Belgorod (top)	G-2	H50
Belgrade (top)	C-1	H37
Belleau Wood	K-5	H45
Benadir (left)	G-6	H41
Benevento	G-4	H13
Beneventum	E-4	H 9
Benghazi (top)	E-4	H50
Benin, Kingdom of	F-8	H40
Berbers	C-4	H12
Berchtesgaden (top)	D-3	H48
Beresina River	L-3	H31
Berlin	F-3	H44
Bernicia	R-14	H14
Berry	P-16	H22
Berwick	B-2	H24
Bessarabia	D-1	H37
Bethlehem (top)	D-4	H 6
Biafra	B-3	H57
Biak (bottom)	D-4	H50
Bias Bay (bottom)	D-4	H48
Bikini	L-5	H55
Bilbao (top)	B-3	H48
Birmingham	G-5	H36
Bithynia	N-6	H 8
Bizerte (top)	D-4	H50
Björkö	G-2	H44
Blenheim	J-4	H26
Blois	J-10	H22
Bodh Gaya	E-2	H18
Boeotia (bottom)	C-2	H 6
Bohemia	E-4	H19
Bohemia-Moravia (Protectorate) (top)	D-2	H48
Bokhara	B-7	H38
Bolivia (right)		H33
Bornu	Map 15	VIII
Borobudur	F-4	H18
Borodino	N-2	H31
Bosnia	F-4	H44
Botany Bay	D-3	H42
Boulogne	F-3	H31
Bourbon	H-22	Q16
Boyacá (right)		H33
Brandenburg	E-3	H25
Brazil		H33
Breitenfeld	E-3	H25
Brest Litovsk	G-3	H44
Bretigny	Q-15	H22
Bretton Woods	F-33	H60
Britannia (Roman)		H14
Brittany	G-9	H22
Brundisium	F-4	H 9
Brunswick (top)	C-2	H35
Brussels	E-3	H51
Bucharest	G-4	H46
Buda (top)	C-1	H37
Budapest	G-4	H46
Buenos Aires		H33
Bukovina (bottom)	D-1	H37
Bulawayo (left)	F-9	H41
Bulgaria (bottom)	E-2	H17
Bulgarian Empire (bottom)	E-2	H15
Bulgars	Map 8	IV
Bulge, Battle of the (top)	D-2	H50
Burgos (top)	B-3	H48
Burgundians	F-2,D-3	H11
Burgundy	X-22	H22
Burgundy, Upper	M-4	H13
Burma	E-2	H18
Burma Road (bottom)	B-4	H48
Bursa (Brusa)	D-1	H37
Buwaihids	Map 9	V
Byzantine Empire		H16
Byzantium	M-6	H 8
Cádiz	J-3	H23
Caesarea (bottom inset)		H17
Cairo	S-4	H49
Cairo, Califate of (top)	J-4	H17
Calais	P-14	H22
Calcutta	E-2	H18
Caledonia	C-1	H13
Cambodia	B-3	H56
Cambodia, Empire of	F-3	H18
Cambrai	C-3	H24
Campo Formio (left)	E-4	H30
Canada		H43
Canal Zone	D-4	H58
Candia (Crete)	H-7	H25
Cannae	F-4	H 9
Canterbury (Cantwarabyrig)	K-8	H14
Caporetto (right)	E-1	H34
Cappadocia	N-7	H 8
Caprivi Zipfel (left)	E-8	H41
Capua (top)	E-2	H17
Carabobo (right)		H33
Caracas		H33
Carchemish (top)	E-1	H 6
Carlsbad	E-3	H32
Caroline Is. (bottom)	E-3	H50
Carolingian Kingdom		H13
Carpatho-Ukraine (top)	E-3	H48
Cartagena (Colombia)		H33
Cartagena (Spain)	D-5	H44
Carthage	Map 1	I
Casablanca (top)	C-4	H50
Castelfidardo (right)	F-3	H34
Castile	C-4	H19
Castle and Leon	Map 10	V
Catalan Counties (top)	C-2	H17
Catalonia (top)	C-3	H48
Catalonian Fields	C-3	H11
Cawnpore	D-2	H18
Celts	Map 2	I
Central American Confederation (right)		H33
Cerignola	F-5	H24
Ceuta (bottom)	B-3	H15
Chad	B-3	H57
Chaeronea (bottom)	C-2	H 6
Chaghatai, Khanate of	D-1	H18
Chalcidice (bottom)	C-1	H 6
Chalcis (bottom)	C-2	H 6
Châlons	C-3	H11
Chalukya (bottom)	C-4	H10
Champa (bottom)	G-4	H10
Champagne	K-9	H22
Changkufeng (bottom)	F-2	H48
Château-Cambrésis	C-3	H24
Château-Thierry	K-5	H45
Chaumont	C-4	H32
Chavin	Map 1	I
Chemin des Dames	K-5	H45
Chengtu (Chengdu)	F-2	H18
Chenla (bottom)	G-4	H10
Cherchel (bottom)	C-3	H15
Chibcha	Map 10	V
Chile		H33
Chimu	Map 9	V
Ch'in (Qin) Empire	F-2	H 7
China	F-2,G-4	H 7
China	G-3	H10
Chinese Eastern R.R. (bottom)	D-2	H48
Chinese Rep. (right)	G-3	H41
Chioggia (left)	E-2	H34
Chios (bottom)	D-2	H 6
Chola	Map 9	V
Chosen (right)	H-3	H41
Choson	G-2	H 7
Chungking (bottom)	C-4	H48
"Cibola"	B-3	H23
Cid, Dominion of the (top)	B-3	H17
Cilicia (bottom)	G-2	H 5
Circassians	K-5	H32
Cisalpine Republic (Italian Rep.) (left)	D-4	H30
Ciudad de los Reyes (Lima) (left)		H33
Clermont (top)	C-1	H17
Cleve (right)	B-2	H30
Coimbra	C-4	H19
Colchis	O-6	H 8
Cologne (right)	B-3	H30
Colombia (right)		H33
Compiegne	K-5	H45
Confederation of the Rhine		H31
Congo Free State	N-20	H40
Constantinople	E-1	H37
Constantinople, Empire of	F-4	H19
Coral Sea (bottom)	E-4	H50
Cordova, Caliphate of	C-5	H13
Corfu (Kerkyra)	F-5	H46
Corinth (bottom)	C-3	H 6
Corsica (bottom)	B-2	H17
Costa Rica (right)		H33
Courland, Duchy of	G-2	H27
Covadonga (bottom)	B-2	H15
Coventry (top)	C-2	H50
Cracow, Rep. of	G-3	H32
Crécy	Q-14	H22
Cremona	D-4	H19
Crete (bottom)	B-3	H 6
Crete (top)	F-4	H50
Crimea	A-5	H38
Crimean Khanate	J-4	H24
Croatia (top)	F-2	H17
Crusades		H17
Ctesiphon (bottom)	D-3	H10
Cuba	D-2	H58
Cumae	D-4	H 9
Cumans	F-4	H19
Custozza (right)	D-2	H34
Cuzco		H33
Cyclades (bottom)	D-3	H 6
Cyprus, Kingdom of (bottom)	G-3	H17
Cyrenaica (left)	E-3	H41
Cyzicus (bottom)	E-1	H 6
Czechoslovakia	F-4	H46
Dacia	M-6	H 8
Dagestan	A-6	H38
Dakar	P-5	H49
Dalmatia	L-6	H 8
Damascus (top)	E-3	H 6
Damascus (bottom)	F-3	H15
Damascus, Emirates of (bottom inset)		H17
Damietta (bottom)	G-4	H17
Danelaw, The	S-15	H14
Danes	F-1	H13
Danishmand Emirate (top)	K-3	H17
Danzig	J-3	H51
Danzig, Republic of	K-1	H31
Dara (Daras)	G-4	H12
Dardanelles	G-5	H44
Darfur	Map 16	VIII
Dauphiné	X-23	H22
Decelea (bottom)	C-2	H 6
Delagoa Bay (left)	F-9	H41
Delhi	D-2	H18
Delhi Sultanate	Map 10	V
Delos (bottom)	D-3	H 6
Delphi (bottom)	C-2	H 6
Denmark	E-3	H19
Denmark & Norway, Kingdom of	D-2	H24
Derbent (bottom)	G-2	H15
Dettingen (right)	E-3	H30
Dien Bien Phu	E-4	H55
Dilmun	H-5	H 4
Dobrudja (bottom)	D-1	H37
Dodecanese (bottom)	D-2	H37
Dominican Republic	E-3	H58
Domremy	X-21	H22
Don Cossacks	H-3	H38
Dongola, Kingdom of	F-5	H15
Doris (bottom)	E-3	H 6
Dorylaeum (top)	H-3	H17
Drepanum	D-6	H 9
Dresden	H-3	H31
Dumbarton Oaks	E-4	H60
Dunkerque (top)	D-2	H50
Düppel (top)	C-1	H35
Durazzo	F-4	H44
Durban (left)	F-9	H41
Dutch East Indies (right)	G-6	H41
Dvin (top)	G-2	H15
Dzungars	Map 15	VIII
East Africa Protectorate (left)	F-6	H41
East Anglia	P-11	H14
East Frankish Kdm.	N-2	H13
East Friesland	D-3	H27
East Goths	J-3, F-3	H11
East Prussia (top)	E-2	H48
East Germany ("Dem." Rep.)	F-3	H52
Eastern Roman Empire		H11,H12
Eastern Rumelia (bottom)	D-1	H37
Eastern Turks	Map 7	IV
Ebia	A-5	H 4
Ecbatana (bottom)	D-2	H 5
Ecuador (right)		H33
Edessa, County of (bottom inset)	A-2	H17
Edinburgh	B-2	H24
Egypt (ancient)	C-4	H 4
Eire	C-3	H51
El Alamein (top)	F-4	H50
Elam	H-4	H 4
Elba	E-5	H32
Elea	E-4	H 9
Elis (bottom)	B-3	H 6
Enewetak	L-5	H55
Ephesus (top)	B-2	H 8
Epirus (bottom)	B-2	H 6
Epirus, Despotate of	F-4	H19
Erfurt (top)	C-2	H35
Eritrea (left)	F-5	H41
Eskishehr (top)	E-2	H37
Essen (top)	B-2	H35
Essex (East Saxonia)	O-12	H14
Esthonia	F-3	H19
Estonia	G-3	H46
Ethiopia	Q-18	H40
Etruria	C-3	H 9
Etruria, Kingdom of (left)	E-5	H30
Euboea (bottom)	C-2	H 6
Eupen	M-4	H45
Eylau, Preussisch	K-3	H31
Falkland Islands (right)		H33
Fashoda (left)	F-5	H41
Fatimite Caliphate (top)	J-4	H17
Ferrara, Duchy of (left)	B-3	H41
Fez (left)	B-3	H41
Fez and Morocco	B-7	H24
Fezzan (left)	D-4	H41
Finland (top)	F-2	H50
Finns	Map 8	IV
Fiume	F-4	H46
Flanders	Q-14	H22
Fleurus (left)	C-3	H30
Flodden	B-2	H24
Florence, Republic of (left)	D-3	H34
Fontainbleau	F-4	H31
Fontenoy (Belgium)	G-3	H26
Fontenoy (France)	J-1	H13
Formosa	G-2	H18
Fort Duquesne	K-12	H26
France		H22
Franche Comté	D-4	H24
Franconia	D-4	H19
Frank Kingdoms	C-3	H12
Frankfurt (Frankfort)	D-3	H32
Frankish Kingdom	D-3	H13
French Empire		H31
Friedland	K-3	H31
Frisians	C-2	H12
Funan	G-4	H10
Funj	Map 15	VIII
Füssen	E-4	H27
Fustat (bottom)	F-3	H15
Gaeta (left)	E-4	H34
Galatia	N-7	H 8
Galicia	G-8	H28
Galicia & Asturias, Kingdom of	B-4	H13
Galilee (top)	D-3	H 6
Gallia Cisalpina	B-2	H 9
Gambela (left)	F-6	H41
Gascony	B-6	H22
Gastein (top)	D-3	H35
Gaugamela	D-2	H 8
Gaul	K-6	H 8
Gaza (top)	D-4	H 6
Gaza Strip	L-6	H54
Gedrosia (bottom)	F-3	H 5
Gela	E-6	H 9
General-Gouvernement	G-3	H51
Geneva	E-4	H46
Genoa, Republic of (left)	C-2	H34
Georgia (Russia)	A-6	H38
Georgia, Kingdom of (bottom)	J-2	H17
Gepids	G-3	H11
German Confederation (top)		H35
German East Africa (left)	F-7	H41
German Empire (top)		H35
German Southwest Africa (left)	D-9	H41
Germania	L-5	H 8
Germany	E,F-3	H52
Ghana, Kingdom of	E-8	H40
Ghassanid Kingdom	F-4	H12
Ghazna	Map 9	V
Ghent (top)	A-2	H35
Gibraltar	F-6	H26
Gnesen	E-3	H19
Godesberg (top)	C-2	H48
Golan Heights	M-5	H54
Golden Chersonese (top)	G-4	H10
Golden Horde, Khanate of the	C-1	H18
Goshen (top)	B-4	H 6
Goths	F-2,J-3,B-4	H11
Granada	B-6	H24
Great Britain & Ireland, Kingdom of	E-3	H26
Great Khan Empire (Yuan Dynasty)	Map 11	VI
Greece	G-5	H46
Greece, Ancient (bottom)		H 6
Greenland	M-2	H49
Grossjägermdorf	G-3	H27
Guadalajara (left)		H33
Guadalcanal (bottom)	E-4	H50
Guadalete (bottom)	B-3	H15
Guatemala		H33
Gupta Empire (bottom)	E-3	H10
Gurganj	H-2	H15
Gurjara-Pratihara	Map 8	IV
Guthrum, Kdm. of	T-16	H14
Guyenne	J-11	H22
Habbaniya (top)	H-4	H50
Habsburg Dominions		H25
Hadhramaut	H-5	H15
Hadrian's Wall	C-2	H14
Hadrianopolis (Adrianople)	E-2	H15
Hafsids (bottom)	B-3	H17
Hague, The	E-3	H44
Haiphong (right)	B-1	H56
Haiti (right)		H33
Halicarnassus (bottom)	E-3	H 6
Hamburg	E-3	H27
Hammadites (top)	C-3	H17
Han Empire (top)	G-3	H10
Hangchow	F-2	H18
Hanifa (top)	G-4	H15
Hankow (bottom)	D-3	H48
Hanoi (right)	B-1	H56
Hanover (top)	C-2	H35
Hanseatic League		H21
Harappa	C-3	H 7
Harbin (right)	H-3	H41
Harran (bottom)	G-3	H15
Harsha's Empire (bottom)	C-4	H10
Hasa (right)	D-4	H41
Hastenbeck (right)	E-1	H30
Hastings	C-2	H22
Hatay (top)	F-4	H48
Hattin (Hittin) (bottom inset)		H17
Hattusas	D-2	H 4
Hausaland	Map 16	VIII
Havana (La Habana)		H33
Hawaiian Islands	F-4	H49
Hawazin (top)	G-4	H15
Hazaraspids	H-5	H19
Hebron (top)	D-4	H 6
Heilan Japan	Map 8	IV
Hejaz (right)	C-4	H41
Helgoland	E-3	H44
Heliopolis (top)	B-4	H 6
Hellas (bottom)		H 6
Helvetian Rep. (left)	D-4	H30
Heraclea	F-4	H 9
Herat (top)	J-3	H15
Herculaneum	E-4	H 9
Hesse (top)	C-2	H34
Himera	D-6	H 9
Himyar	Map 4	II
Hippo Regius	D-5	H11
Hira (top)	G-3	H15
Hiroshima (bottom)	D-2	H50
Hispania (Spain)	J-6	H 8
Hispaniola (Española) (left)		H33
Hittite Empire	D-2	H 4
Ho Chi Minh Trail (right)	B-2	H56
Höchstädt (right)	F-5	H30
Hohenlinden (left)	E-4	H30
Hohenzollern	C-3	H35
Holstein (top)	C-2	H35
Holy Roman Empire	D-4	H19
Homs (top)	F-3	H15
Honduras (right)		H33
Hong Kong	F-2	H18
Hotel de Ville (bottom)	D-2	H29
Hsiung-nu (Huns)	F-2	H10
Huari	Map 8	IV
Hubertusburg	E-3	H27
Hudson's Bay Company		H43
Hué (right)	B-2	H56
Hungary	E-4	H19
Hungary, Kingdom of	E-3	H35
Huns		H11,H18
Hydaspes River	G-2	H 8
Iceland (top)	B-1	H50
Iconium, Sult. of	H-3	H17
Ife	F-8	H40
Ilium (Troy) (bottom)	E-2	H 6
Ilkhanate	Map 11	VI
Illyrian Provinces	H-4	H31
Illyricum	F-4	H11
Imphal (bottom)	B-2	H50
Inca Empire	Map 10	V
Inchon	D-2	H56
India	E-3	H10
Indian Empire (right)	E-4	H41
Indonesia	F-7	H55
Indus Valley Civilization	C-3	H 7
Inuit	Map 10	V
Iona	F-5	H14
Ionia (bottom)	E-2	H 6
Ionian Islands	F-6	H32
Ipsus	C-2	H 8
Iran	H-3	H54
Ireland	D-3	H52
Iroquois	Map 10	V
Irish Free State	C-3	H46
Isfahan (Ispahan)	C-2	H18
Islam		H15
Israel, Kingdom of (top)	D-4	H 6
Israel, Republic of	L-6	H54
Issus	C-2	H 8
Istakhr (top)	H-4	H15
Italian East Africa	T-5	H49
Italian Republic (1803) (left)	D-4	H30
Itil	B-3	H38
Iviza (bottom)	C-3	H15
Ivry	C-4	H24
Iwo Jima (bottom)	E-2	H50
Izapan	Map 3	II
Jacobins, les (bottom)	C-1	H29
Jagatai Khanate	Map 11	VI
Jammu & Kashmir	B-3	H55
Jankau	E-4	H25
Japan	G-2	H18
Jassy	H-7	H38
Java Sea (bottom)	C-4	H50
Jena	H-3	H31
Jerba	K-3	H23
Jericho (top)	D-4	H 6
Jerusalem (top)	B-3	H 6
Jerusalem, Kingdom of (bottom inset)		H17
Jordan	E-3	H54
Juan-Juan (Avars)	Map 6	III
Jubaland (left)	G-6	H41
Juchen	Map 9	V
Judah (top)	D-4	H 6
Jülich (right)	B-3	H30
Jutes	D-1	H11
Jwen-Jwen	Map 1	I
Kabul	J-3	H15
Kaifeng (bottom)	D-3	H48
Kairwan (top)	D-3	H17
Kalisch	J-3	H31
Kalmar	F-2	H24
Kama Bulgaria	H-3	H19
Kamakura Japan	Map 10	V
Kamerun (left)	D-6	H41
Kandahar	J-3	H15
Kanem-Bornu	G-7	H40
Kapilavastu	E-2	H18
Karafuto (right)	J-3	H41
Karakorum	F-1	H18
Karbala (Kerbela) (top)	G-3	H15
Karkar (top)	E-2	H 6
Kars	A-6	H38
Kashmir, Jammu &	B-3	H55
Kasserine (top)	D-4	H50
Kassites	G-3	H 4
Katanga	C-4	H57
Kazan, Khanate of	F-2	H38
Kent (Cantia)	P-12	H14
Kenya	C-3	H57
Kerch (bottom)	E-1	H37
Khalkha Mongols	Map 13	VII
Khanate of the Golden Horde	Map 11	VI
Khanbalik	F-2	H18
Kharkov (top)	G-3	H50
Khartoum (bottom)	E-4	H37
Khazar Empire	B-3	H38
Khelat (bottom)	J-3	H17
Khitans	Map 8	IV
Khiva	B-7	H38
Khmer Empire	F-3	H18
Khorasan (top)	H-3	H15
Khwarizm (bottom)	H-2	H15
Khyber Pass	D-2	H18
Kiaochow (right)	G-4	H41
Kiel Canal	E-3	H44
Kiev	A-2	H38
Kievan Rus	E-3	H16
Kimberley (left)	E-9	H41
Kinda (top)	G-4	H15
Kiska (bottom)	F-1	H50

INDEX Contd.

Index Ref.	Plate No.
Knossos (bottom) B-3	H 6
Koguryo .... Map 7	IV
Königgrätz (top) D-2	H35
Königsberg F-3	H25
Korea (left)	H56
Koryo .... Map 9	V
Kossovo (top) D-1	H37
Kronstadt G-3	H44
Kuchuk-Kainarji J-7	H38
Kufa G-3	H15
Kunersdorf F-3	H27
Kunming (bottom) C-4	H48
Kurds F-2	H54
Kursk (top) G-3	H50
Kushan Empire (top) .... Map 4	II
Kut al Imara (bottom) F-2	H37
Kuwait G-4	H54
Kwajalein (bottom) F-3	H50
Kwangchowwan (right) G-4	H41
La Plata, Rio de	H33
La Rochelle B-4	H25
Lado (left) F-6	H41
Ladysmith (left) F-9	H41
Lake Kingdom .... Map 13	VII
Lakhmid Kdm. (top) G-3	H15
Langensalza (top) C-2	H35
Langkasuka G-4	H10
Languedoc K12	H22
Laos (right) A-2	H56
Lashio (bottom) B-4	H48
Latin Empire (bottom) E-3	H17
Latium D-4	H 9
Latvia G-3	H46
Lausanne E-4	H46
Lebanon M-5	H54
Ledo (bottom) B-2	H50
Leipzig H-3	H31
Lemberg G-4	H44
Leningrad (top) G-2	H50
Leoben (left) F-4	H30
Leon C-4	H19
Lepanto (top) D-2	H37
Lesbos (bottom) E-2	H 6
Lesser Armenia (bottom inset)	H17
Leyte (bottom) D-3	H50
Libya B-2	H57
Liechtenstein (left) E-6	H30
Ligurian Rep. (left) D-5	H30
Lima	H33
Lindisfarne J-6	H14
Lingayen Gulf (bottom) C-3	H50
Lithuania G-3	H46
Lithuania, Grand Duchy of H-3	H24
Lithuanians E-2	H12
Liu Sung .... Map 6	III
Livonia C-2	H28
Lobito Bay (left) D-8	H41
Lodz C-1	H45
Lombard Kingdom D-3	H12
Lombard League	H19
Lombards E-2	H11
Lombardy-Venetia E-4	H32
Loninium (London) E-4	H14
Loos K-4	H45
Lorraine, Duchy of .. H-4	H26
Lotharingia K-1	H13
Louisbourg M-9	H26
Lübeck E-3	H25
Luoyand (Loyang) (top) G-3	H10
Lublin G-3	H24
Lucca (left) D-3	H34
Lunéville (left) D-4	H30
Luristan F-2	H37
Lusitania J-7	H 8
Lützen E-3	H25
Luxemburg (top) B-3	H35
Luzon (bottom) D-3	H50
Lydia B-2	H 5
Macedonia (bottom) .. B-1	H 6
Madagascar R-19	H40
Madain (Ctesiphon) (top) G-3	H15
Madjapahit Kingdom G-4	H18
Madrid B-5	H24
Mafeking (left)	H41
Magadha .... Map 2	I
Magar .... Map 8	IV
Magdeburg E-3	H25
Magenta (right) C-2	H34
Magnano (left) E-4	H30
Magnesia (bottom) .. E-3	H 6
Magyars (600 A.D.)	H12
Mahdist State Q-18	H40
Mahedia (top) C-2	H37
Maine (France) C-3	H22
Mainz (left) D-4	H20
Maipú (right)	H33
Majapahit .... Map 11	VI
Malagasy .... Map 7	IV
Malaysia E-6	H55
Mali, Empire of E-8	H40
Malmedy M-4	H45
Malolos (right) G-5	H41
Malplaquet G-4	H26
Malta E-6	H24
Malta (top) E-4	H50
Mameluke Sultanate .... Map 11	VI
Manchester G-5	H38
Manchu (Ch'ing) Dynasty .... Map 15	VIII
Manchus .... Map 12	VII
Manchukuo (bottom) E-2	H48
Manila (bottom) D-3	H50
Mantinea (bottom) .. C-3	H 6
Mantua (left) D-3	H34
Manzikert (top) L-3	H17
Maori .... Map 9	V
Maragha (bottom) .. K-3	H17
Marathas .... Map 16	VIII
Marathon (bottom) .. C-2	H 6
Marcomanni L-6	H 8
Marengo (left) D-5	H30
Mareth (top) E-4	H50
Mari B-5	H 4
Mariana Islands (bottom) E-3	H50
Marinids .... Map 12	VI
Mark (right) C-2	H30
Marne River L-5	H45
Marrakesh C-5	H19
Marshall Islands (bottom) F-3	H50
Matabeleland (left) .. E-8	H41
Mataram .... Map 2	II
Mauretania J-7	H 8
Mayan States .... Map 4	II
Mecca (top) G-4	H15
Mecklenburg D-2	H35
Median Empire (bottom)	H 5
Medina (top) G-4	H15
Megara (bottom) C-2	H 6
Megiddo (top) D-3	H 6
Memel (top) D-2	H48
Memphis C-4	H 4
Mentana (right) E-3	H34
Mercia O-11	H14
Merj Dabik (top) E-2	H37
Meroe B-3	H 7
Mersen N-2	H13
Mesopotamia (top).. B-5	H 4
Messana E-5	H 9
Messenia (bottom) .. B-3	H 6
Metz (top) B-3	H35
Meuse River L-5	H45
Mexico	H33
Midway (bottom) G-2	H50
Milan (left) C-2	H34
Minaean Civilization .... Map A	H 3
Ming Dynasty .... Map 12	VI
Minoan-Mycenaean Domain B-2	H 4
Minorca G-5	H26
Missolonghi (bottom) C-2	H37
Mitanni F-2	H 4
Mixtec-Zapotec . Map 11	VI
Moab (top) D-4	H 6
Moche .... Map 4	II
Modena, Duchy of (left) D-2	H34
Moesia M-6	H 8
Mogul Empire .... Map D	H 3
Mohacs (top) C-1	H37
Mohenjo-Daro C-4	H 7
Moldavia D-1	H37
Mongolia R-3	H60
Mongols F-1	H18
Monomotapa G-9	H40
Mons K-4	H45
Montenegro F-4	H44
Montevideo	H33
Montferrat D-5	H24
Moravian Kingdom.. N-4	H13
Morea L-6	H26
Moroccan Empire .... Map 14	VII
Morocco (left) B-3	H41
Morotai (bottom) D-3	H50
Moscow (top) G-2	H50
Moscow, Principality of F-2	H38
Mosul H-5	H19
Mound Builders . Map 8	IV
Mukden (top) H-3	H41
Munich (top) D-3	H48
Murmansk (top) G-1	H50
Muscovy (inset) E-1	H38
Mutina C-2	H 9
Mycenae A-2	H 4
Mylae E-5	H 9
Mysia (bottom) B-2	H 8
Nagasaki (bottom) .. D-2	H50
Nanchao E-2	H18
Nanking (bottom) ... D-3	H48
Nantes B-4	H24
Naples, Kingdom of (left) F-4	H34
Nara G-2	H18
Narbonne D-4	H13
Narvik (top) E-1	H50
Nassau (top) C-2	H35
Nationalist China .. S-4	H60
Navarino (bottom) .. D-2	H37
Navarre C-4	H19
Naxos (left) F-3	H17
Nazareth (top) D-3	H 6
Nazca .... Map 3	II
Neanderthal (top)	H 2
Negropont G-6	H24
Nehavend (top) G-3	H15
Nejd (right) D-4	H41
Neuchâtel (top) B-3	H35
Neustria D-3	H13
New Castilia (Peru) (left)	H33
New Granada (left)	H33
New Guinea (bottom) D-4	H50
New Spain (left)	H33
Newfoundland G-3	H59
New Zealand	H42
Nicaea, Empire of (top) F-3	H17
Nicaragua (right)	H33
Nice (right) B-3	H34
Nicomedia (top) J-2	H17
Nimwegan (right) .. A-2	H30
Nineveh (top) F-2	H 5
Nishapur H-3	H15
Nisibis (bottom) F-2	H37
Nok .... Map 2	I
Nomonhan (bottom). D-2	H48
Noricum L-6	H 8
Normandy (top) C-3	H50
Normandy, Duchy of B-3	H22
Normans (top) F-2	H17
Northern Ireland ... D-3	H52
Northern Wei Dynasty .... Map 6	III
North German Confederation .. N-10	H35
Northumbria O-11	H14
Northwest Territory	H43
Novara (right) C-2	H34
Novgorod D-1	H38
Novi (left) D-5	H30
Numidia K-7	H33
Nürnberg (top) D-3	H48
Nystad H-4	H38
Oder River F-3	H53
Odessa (top) G-3	H50
Offa's Dyke C-2	H13
Ogaden (bottom) B-3	H50
Ohod, Mt. (top) G-4	H15
Oirat Mongols .. Map 13	VII
Okinawa (bottom) .. D-2	H50
Oldenburg (top) C-2	H35
Olduvai (top)	H 2
Oliva E-4	H45
Olmec .... Map 1	I
Olmütz (top) E-3	H35
Olympus (bottom) .. C-1	H 6
Omani Zanzibar . Map 15	VIII
Omayyad Empire (bottom)	H15
Omdurman (bottom). E-4	H37
Oran (top) D-4	H50
Orange, Princ. of ... C-5	H34
Orange Free State (left) E-9	H41
Orel (top) G-2	H50
Orléans W-22	H27
Ortuqids (bottom) .. H-3	H17
Ostend K-4	H45
Ostrogoths (East Goths) J-3,F-3	H11
Ostrolenka A-4	H38
Ottoman Empire	H37
Oudenarde G-3	H26
Outer Mongolia (right) G-3	H41
Oyo .... Map 10	V
Pacific Islands, Territory of the J-6	H55
Paekche (top) H-3	H10
Pakistan A-4	H55
Palatinate (top) B-3	H35
Palestine (top)	H 6
Pallava (bottom) E-4	H10
Palmyra (top) E-2	H 6
Palos J-3	H23
Panamá	H33
P'anmunjóm D-4	H56
Pannonia L-6	H 8
Papal States (right) . E-3	H34
Paracas .... Map 2	I
Paraguay (right)	H33
Paramushiru (bottom) E-1	H50
Parhae .... Map 8	IV
Parma, Duchy of (right) C-2	H34
Parnassus (bottom).. C-2	H 6
Parthian Emp. (top) . D-3	H 8
Passarowitz G-5	H27
Passchendaele K-4	H45
Pataliputra E-2	H 7
Pavia E-3	H13
Pearl Harbor (bottom) G-3	H50
Pechenegs A-3	H38
Peipus, Lake C-1	H38
Peking (Beijing) F-2	H18
Peleliu (bottom) D-3	H50
Pella (top) C-1	H 6
Peloponnesus (bottom) C-3	H 6
Pergamum M-7	H 8
Pernambuco (Recife)	H33
Persepolis (bottom). E-2	H 5
Persia .... Map 16	VIII
Persian Empire	H 8
Persian Gulf G-4	H54
Persis (bottom) E-3	H 5
Peru (right)	H33
Petra (top) D-4	H 6
Philippines, Republic of G-5	H55
Philippine Sea (bottom) D-3	H50
Philistia (top) D-4	H 6
Phoenicia (top) D-2	H 6
Phrygian Kingdom .. C-2	H 5
Piacenza (top) D-3	H17
Pichincha (right)	H33
Piombino (left) D-3	H34
Piraeus (bottom) C-2	H 6
Pisa (left) D-4	H19
Plassey E-2	H18
Plataea (bottom) C-2	H 6
Plevna (Pleven) G-4	H44
Ploesti (top) F-3	H50
Podolia H-4	H25
Poitiers O-16	H22
Poland, Partition of	H28
Polish Corridor (top). D-2	H48
Pollentia A-2	H 9
Polovtsi D-2	H38
Poltava J-5	H38
Polynesians .... Map 3	II
Pomerania E-3	H16
Pompeii E-4	H 9
Pontus N-6	H 8
Port Arthur F-7	H38
Portugal A-6	H19
Portugal, County of (top) A-2	H19
Prague E-3	H25
Pressburg J-4	H31
Preveza (top) D-2	H37
Prome B-4	H24
Provence E-4	H13
Prussia, Kingdom of. C-2	H35
Prussians F-3	H19
Przemyśl G-3	H44
Pskov C-1	H38
Ptolemaic Kingdom . B-2	H 7
Pueblo Dwellers. Map 11	VI
Puerto Rico	H33
Purushapura E-3	H10
Pusan B-2	H56
Pydna (bottom) C-1	H 6
Pyongyang D-2	H56
Pyramids (top) B-5	H 6
Qadisiya (top) G-3	H15
Qain H-3	H15
Quadi L-6	H 8
Quebec M-10	H26
Quemoy F-4	H55
Quito	H33
Ragusa, Republic of. F-5	H25
Rai H-5	H15
Ramillies H-3	H26
Rangoon (bottom) .. B-3	H50
Raqqa (bottom) F-3	H15
Rastatt H-4	H26
Ravenna E-4	H11
Ravensberg (right) . D-1	H30
Regensburg (Ratisbon) H-4	H31
Reichstadt F-3	H44
Reykjavík B-2	H52
Rhaetia K-6	H 8
Rhineland (top) C-2	H48
Rhodes (bottom) F-3	H17
Rhodesia (left) E-8	H41
Riga G-3	H46
Rivoli (left) E-4	H30
Rocoux (right) A-3	H30
Romagna (right) D-2	H34
Roman Empire	H 8
Rome (Roma) D-4	H 9
Roncesvalles (bottom) B-2	H15
Rossbach E-3	H27
Roussillon C-5	H25
Rozwi .... Map 15	VIII
Rubicon (Rubico) .. D-2	H 9
Ruhr (top) D-2	H50
Rum, Sultanate of . H-3	H17
Rumania G-4	H44
Russian Empire	H38
Ryswick C-3	H26
Sabaean Kingdom .. C-3	H 7
Sabines (Sabini) D-3	H 9
Sadowa (top) D-3	H35
Safavid Empire . Map 13	VII
Sahel B-3	H57
Saigon (right) B-4	H56
St. Albans C-3	H19
St. Mihiel L-5	H45
St. Peter, Patrimony of (top) E-2	H17
St. Petersburg J-4	H38
St. Quentin K-5	H45
Saipan (bottom) E-3	H50
Sakaria River (bottom) E-1	H37
Sakas D-1	H 7
Sakhalin Island G-6	H38
Saladin, Sultanate of (bottom) G-4	H17
Salamis (bottom) ... C-3	H 6
Salerno (top) E-4	H50
Salian Franks C-2	H11
Saluzzo (left) B-2	H34
Salzburg (left) E-4	H30
Samaria (top) D-3	H 6
Samarkand D-2	H18
Samarra (bottom).. G-3	H15
Samartians .... Map 3	II
Samo, Kingdom of .. D-3	H13
Samori's Empire.. N-18	H40
San Francisco C-4	H60
San Salvador (left)	H33
San Stefano G-4	H44
Santa Fé, Audienca of (top)	H33
Santa Fé de Bogotá (left)	H33
Santa María del Buen Aire (left)	H33
Santiago	H33
Santo Domingo (left)	H33
São Sebastião do Rio de Janeiro (left)	H33
Saragossa C-4	H19
Saragossa, Emirate of (top) .. B-2	H17
Sarai D-3	H38
Sarajevo F-4	H44
Sardinia J-5	H26
Sardinia, Kingdom of (right) B-2,C-4	H34
Sardis (bottom) B-2	H 5
Sarmatia N-5	H 8
Sassanid Empire (bottom) D-3	H10
Sasun (bottom) F-2	H37
Savoy H-4	H26
Saxa Rubra B-4	H 9
Saxons D-2	H11
Saxony J-2	H27
Scandinavians .. Map 8	IV
Scapa Flow A-1	H45
Schleswig (top) C-1	H35
Schmalkalden E-3	H24
Scotland B-2	H24
Scots B-2	H12
Scythians B-1	H 8
Sedan (top) B-3	H35
Segu .... Map 16	VIII
Seistan J-3	H15
Seleucid Empire C-2	H 7
Seljuk Turks (top) .. L-3	H17
Senussi (bottom) .. D-3	H37
Seoul B-2	H56
Serbia E-4	H19
Serbia G-4	H44
Sevastopol A-5	H38
Seville A-6	H24
Shang China G-4	H 7
Shanghai (top) D-3	H50
Shemakha H-4	H19
Shimonoseki (right). H-4	H41
Shirvan H-4	H19
Siam .... Map 13	VII
Sibir, Khanate of .. K-2	H38
Sicily, Kingdom of . J-6	H26
Sidon (top) D-3	H 6
Siena, (left) D-3	H34
Silesia F-3	H35
Silk Route F-2,3	H10
Silla .... Map 7	IV
Simla N-4	H59
Sinai Pen. (top) C-5	H 6
Singapore (bottom). C-3	H50
Sis (bottom inset)	H17
Sivas (top) K-3	H17
Slavs .... Map 7	IV
Slovakia (top) D-3	H48
Smyrna (Izmir) G-5	H19
Sogdiana F-2	H 8
Soissons J-1	H13
Sokoto P-18	H40
Solferino (right) D-2	H34
Solomon Islands (bottom) E-4	H50
Solomon's Kingdom (top) D-3	H 6
Somme River K-5	H45
Songhay Empire .. F-7	H40
Sorbs F-2	H13
South Africa, Union of E-10	H41
South Manchuria R.R. (bottom) E-2	H48
Spain, Kingdom of . B-6	H35
Spanish Main (left)	H33
Spanish March D-4	H13
Spanish Netherlands C-3	H25
Sparta (bottom) C-3	H 6
Srivijaya F-3	H18
Stalingrad (top) H-3	H50
Stilwell Road (bottom) B-2	H50
Stockach (left) D-4	H30
Stockholm F-2	H27
Stralsund E-3	H25
Strassburg K-1	H13
Strathclyde N-10	H14
Stresa (top) C-3	H48
Stuhlweissenburg .. E-4	H19
Sudetenland (top) .. D-3	H48
Suevi E-2,A-4	H11
Suevian Kingdom .. B-3	H12
Suez Canal K-6	H54
Sui Dynasty .... Map 7	IV
Sumer G-4	H 4
Suren Kingdom . Map 4	II
Susa (bottom) D-2	H 5
Sussex (Suthsaxona) .. O-12	H14
Suzdal D-2	H38
Swabia D-4	H19
Swatow (bottom) ... D-4	H48
Sweden, Kingdom of G-1	H25
Swiss Confederation D-4	H24
Syracuse (Syracusae) E-6	H 9
Syria (Aram) (top).. E-3	H 6
Tabaristan (bottom). H-3	H15
Tagliacozzo E-4	H19
Taif (top) G-4	H15
Tang Dynasty .. Map 7	IV
Tanga (left) F-7	H41
Tangier (top) C-4	H50
Tangut Kingdom .. D-2	H18
Tannu Tuva (bottom) B-1	H50
Tarawa (bottom) ... F-3	H50
Tarentum (Taranto) . F-4	H 9
Targowitz N-11	H28
Tarsus (top) D-1	H 6
Tartars (Tatars) D-2	H38
Taxila D-1	H 7
Tehran H-2	H54
Telamon C-3	H 9
Tell el Amarna (top). B-6	H 6
Tell el Kebir (bottom) E-2	H37
Temesvar (top) F-4	H35
Temple, le (bottom) . D-2	H29
Teotihuacan .. Map 4	II
Tepanec Empire Map 12	VI
Teplitz H-3	H31
Teruel (top) B-3	H48
Teschen (top) E-2	H48
Teutonic Order, Dominion of the . G-2	H24
Thebes (Egypt) D-5	H 4
Thebes (Greece) (bottom) C-2	H 6
Thermopylae (bottom) C-2	H 6
Thessalonica, Kingdom of F-4	H19
Thessaly (bottom) .. C-2	H 6
Thorn K-10	H28
Thrace M-6	H 8
Thuringians D-2	H12
Tiahuanaco .... Map 7	IV
Tibetans .... Map 8	IV
Ticinus D-3	H 9
Tiflis (bottom) K-2	H17
Tilsit K-3	H31
Timbuktu E-8	H40
Tlemcen A-3	H38
Tmutarakan A-3	H38
Togo (left) C-6	H41
Tokugawa Shogunate G-2	H18
Tokyo (bottom) D-2	H50
Toldeo B-6	H24
Tolentino (left) E-5	H30
Toltec .... Map 8	IV
Toulon (top) D-3	H50
Toulouse D-2	H22
Tournai C-2	H12
Tours (bottom) C-2	H13
Trafalgar, Cape A-6	H27
Trans-Siberian R.R. D-6	H38
Transvaal (left) E-9	H41
Transylvania G-4	H25
Trasimenus, Lake .. D-3	H 9
Treaty Ports (bottom)	H39
Trebizond (bottom). H-2	H17
Trieste F-4	H52
Tripoli (left) D-3	H41
Tripoli, County of (bottom inset)	H17
Trocadero A-6	H32
Troy (Ilium) (bottom). B-2	H 5
Troyes X-21	H22
Truk (bottom) D-3	H50
Tuileries (bottom) .. B-2	H29
Tukulor Empire .. N-18	H40
Tumurid Empire . Map 12	VI
Tunisia (left) D-3	H41
Turin (right) B-2	H34
Turkey (bottom) F-4	H37
Turks .... Map 9	V
Tuscan Presidios .. E-5	H25
Tuscany, Grand Duchy of (right) D-3	H34
Tver F-2	H38
Two Sicilies, Kingdom of (right) . F-5	H34
Tyre (top) D-3	H 6
Uganda	H57
Uihurs .... Map 8	IV
Ujiji L-14	H40
Ulithi (bottom) E-4	H50
Ulm E-4	H25
United Arab Republic D-3	H54
United Nations	H60
United Netherlands . C-3	H25
Uppsala (Upsala) .. E-3	H19
Ur G-4	H 4
Uratu (top) F-2	H 5
Uruguay (right)	H33
Uryankhai (right) .. F-3	H41
Ussuri District G-6	H38
Utrecht H-3	H26
Valais (left) D-4	H30
Valmy (left) C-4	H30
Valparaiso	H33
Van F-2	H37
Vandals F-2,C-5	H11
Van Diemen's Land . D-4	H42
Vendée (left) B-4	H30
Venaissin (top) D-3	H29
Venezuela (right)	H33
Venice, Republic of . E-4	H24
Vercellae B-2	H 9
Verdun (843 A.D.) .. K-1	H13
Verdun (1914-1918). L-5	H45
Verona E-4	H19
Versailles E-4	H46
Versuvius, Mt. E-4	H 9
Vichy (top) D-3	H50
Vienna F-4	H32
Vietnam	H56
Vijayanagara .. Map 12	VI
Vilagos (top) F-3	H35
Villafranca (right) .. D-2	H34
Vilna G-3	H46
Viminacium G-4	H11
Visigothic (West Gothic) Kingdom .. B-3	H12
Visigoths (West Goths) H-3,C-4	H11
Vitoria E-5	H31
Vladimir D-2	H38
Vladivostok G-7	H38
Volga Bulgars, Kingdom of the .. D-2	H38
Volhynia C-2	H38
Volubilis (top) B-3	H15
Voronezh (top) H-2	H50
Wadai (left) D-5	H41
Wagram, Deutsch .. J-4	H31
Wake I. (bottom) ... F-3	H50
Wales B-2	H16
Walili (bottom) B-3	H15
Wallachia D-1	H37
Walvis Bay P-20	H40
Warsaw (top) E-3	H50
Warsaw, Duchy of . K-3	H31
Wasit (bottom)	H15
Waterloo F-3	H31
Watling Street D-3	H14
Wattasids .... Map 13	VII
Wedmore R-16	H14
Weihaiwei (right) .. H-4	H41
Weimar (top) F-3	H46
Wenden H-2	H25
Wessex (West Saxonia) O-12	H14
West Bank M-6	H54
West Frankish Kdm. M-2	H13
West Germany (Fed. Rep.) E-3	H52
West Gothic Kingdom B-3	H12
West Goths H-3,C-4	H11
West Prussia F-7	H35
Western Roman Empire	H11
Western Sahara A-2	H57
Western Turks .. Map 7	IV
Westphalia G-3	H31
Whitby S-14	H14
Wiltzes F-2	H13
Wittenberg E-3	H24
Wittstock E-3	H25
Worms D-3	H20
Württemberg (top) . C-3	H35
Würzburg (left) D-4	H30
Xerxes' Canal (bottom) D-1	H 6
Yalta L-3	H60
Yalu River B-3	H56
Yamato Japan .. Map 7	IV
Yarmuk (top) F-3	H15
Yedisan E-1	H37
Yemama (bottom) .. G-4	H15
Yemen G-6	H54
Yenan (bottom) C-3	H48
York S-15	H14
Ypres K-4	H45
Yue-Chi .... Map 2	I
Yugoslavia F-4	H46
Zab (bottom) G-3	H15
Zaire C-4	H57
Zangids (bottom) .. H-3	H17
Zanj City States . Map 9	V
Zanzibar R-19	H41
Zara F-4	H46
Zayyanids .... Map 13	VII
Zeebrugge K-4	H45
Zeirids (top) C-2	H37
Zenta (bottom) C-1	H37
Zhou (Chou) .. Map 1	I
Zimbabwe (ancient) G-10	H40
Ziyanids (top) A-4	H17
Zululand Q-20	H40
Zürich (left) D-4	H30